THE WARSAW GHETTO

The Warsaw

Ghetto

■ A CHRISTIAN'S TESTIMONY ■

WŁADYSŁAW BARTOSZEWSKI

FOREWORD BY STANISŁAW LEM

TRANSLATED BY STEPHEN G. CAPPELLARI

BEACON PRESS · BOSTON

Beacon Press
25 Beacon Street
Boston, Massachusetts 02108

Beacon Press books
are published under the auspices of
the Unitarian Universalist Association of Congregations.

© 1987 by Beacon Press
Originally published as *Das Warschauer Ghetto — wie es wirklich
war*, © 1983, 1986 by Fischer Taschenbuch Verlag GmbH,
Frankfurt am Main
English translation published by arrangement with Fischer
Taschenbuch Verlag GmbH, Frankfurt am Main

Printed in the United States of America

94 93 92 91 90 89 88   8 7 6 5 4 3 2 1

Text design by Ann Schroeder

Library of Congress Cataloging-in-Publication Data

Bartoszewski, Władysław.
  The Warsaw ghetto.
  Translation of: Das Warschauer Ghetto, wie es
wirklich war. 1983.
  Includes index.
  1. Jews—Poland—Warsaw—Persecutions.
2. Holocaust, Jewish (1939–1945)—Poland—
Warsaw. 3. Warsaw (Poland)—History—Uprising
of 1943. 4. Warsaw (Poland)—Ethnic relations.
I. Title.
DS135.P62W253413 1987 940.53'438 87-42842
ISBN 0-8070-5602-2

Contents

Foreword

In DECEMBER 1942, in great haste, I had to leave the German company in Lvov (then in the "District of Galicia" of the *General Gouvernement*) where I was working because my papers had been "blown." I also saw that I would have to hide the ammunition I had pilfered from the Air Force dump under the wooden stairs in the car repair shop and go into hiding myself before I could obtain new papers. I did not know that at the same time a young man — the same age as I — had founded the Council for Aid to Jews together with several older people in the resistance movement in Warsaw. By then there was no longer a ghetto in Lvov. The miserable shacks and small houses behind the wooden fences — they never put up a real wall in our town — were already empty. At the time I was living in the Lvov Botanical Garden building adjacent to the Lyczakow cemetery, and so I could hear the explosions on those December nights when the German search patrols threw their grenades into the "vaults"[1] where some of the Jews who had fled from the ghetto were still hiding.

There was much I was willing to believe in at the time, above all in the defeat of the Third Reich. But I never thought that, forty-one years later, in Berlin, and in the German language, I would be writing the foreword to a book like this. But as the cynically wise French say, if you live long enough you will experience everything, including its opposite. The Germans, who a half a century ago murdered millions upon millions of Poles, Russians, and Jews using assembly-line technology, are today constructing special underpasses for toads so that the creatures won't be harmed on the highways, and instead of manufacturing Zyklon, with which humans were gassed like bedbugs, today they make vitamin supplements for canaries and goldfish. *Tempora mutantur, nos et mutantur in illis.*

The young man from Warsaw I mentioned earlier was named Władysław Bartoszewski. In the manuscript of this book, he crossed out a name where he lists the founders of *Żegota* — the Council for Aid to Jews. The name was his own. I have, however, denied him the right to such modesty. I have done this not for Professor doctor honoris causa Władysław Bartoszewski, the author of innumerable contemporary essays, histories, and reference works on German-Polish-Jewish relations and on the occupation in Poland, but for the boyish, twenty-one-year-old Władek Bartoszewski, who, soon after his release from Auschwitz, had no other wish than to free Jews before they were murdered by the Germans. At the time the penalty for doing this was death, even if one made only a single, cursory gesture toward aiding a Jew.

I like statistics. But I do not know whether anyone has ever tried to calculate the average chances of survival of the Polish resistance fighters. Without doubt the odds were different, depending on whether these people were active in large cities or in rural areas. The situation, however, in which those who assisted the Jews had to maneuver was unique, and cannot be compared to that of those who fought in the underground.

First of all, one did not risk death for helping Jews everywhere in Nazi-occupied Europe — but in the *General Gouvernement* this was the case up to its final days.

Second, in view of the industrialization of murder by the Germans and the masses of helpless victims, as well as of the continuous decimation of the Polish population during the occupation, it was obvious that only a small fraction of the victims could be saved. In this respect, no one had any illusions from the start.

The daily life of those who helped the Jews teemed with crises, which Bartoszewski discusses in this book. Any kind of planned action that took adequate precaution against informers, extortionists, German traps, and provocations (Bartoszewski says much about these, as well) was out of the question. Whatever the plans and preparation, failure frequently resulted by pure chance, and those who did not retreat in time, who were willing to bear the increased risk, at times shared the Jews' deadly fate.

It is a frightful possibility that our century will enter history as the age of mass murder. Poland was the first European arena of modern genocide. In those days, people wondered why such huge numbers of humans offered no resistance. Several decades later, when Cambodia became the scene of mass killing, and at a time of general world peace, it was already easy to understand that, by itself, even the greatest courage is of no avail against vastly superior forces. Evil is, as we have discovered, more polymorphic, as well as more effective in its murderous actions, than good.

Thus Władysław Bartoszewski was very lucky to have come through the war alive. (What he was fated to experience later is another story.) He was also journalistically active in the underground throughout the war, but he did not become one of our most knowledgeable experts on the occupation until well after the war was over, when he became the historian of the occupation and the investigator of the two Warsaw uprisings — the Jewish uprising of 1943 and the last one, in 1944, when all of Warsaw was destroyed together with half of its population. Even if every one of his essays, chronicles, and books came from a different pen, each work would be a credit to its author. Bartoszewski's great volumes from the war years have become irreplaceable resources for any student of that period. It is gratifying, however, that the young man from the Warsaw of 1942 did not get bogged down in his journalistic efforts of the time, but went on to become a well-known, scholarly, and versatile historian. And reflections of a moralistic nature are rare in his writings. All of his books are addressed to the reader, so that the past will not be forgotten.

Stanisław Lem

THE WARSAW GHETTO

A Christian's Testimony

MORE THAN FORTY YEARS have passed since the events that have been recorded in history under the cynical euphemism "the final solution to the Jewish question." The extent of the unprecedented atrocities and the methods used to carry them out were clearly presented to the world during the great postwar trials of the Nazi criminals; they emerged even more distinctly during the course of the proceedings against Eichmann before the Tribunal in Jerusalem. Much less well known, however, are the problems that beset the cooperation between Jewish and non-Jewish underground organizations in their efforts to bring humanitarian aid to and to save the lives of those threatened with death. At the time, these activities had to be carried out in the utmost secrecy for obvious reasons of security. Some documents pertaining to these organizations were lost during the war, and there are not many people alive today who were directly involved in these efforts. Nevertheless, what they did should never be forgotten. The record of the cooperation between Jews and non-Jews in the territories occupied by Hitler, the record of the secret contacts, which entailed the greatest risk, between the Jewish and Christian underground and the free world (Great Britain, the United States, and what was then Palestine), is of great historical and educational importance.

I am a native of Poland; I was born in Warsaw. In 1939, every tenth inhabitant of Poland and every fourth inhabitant of Warsaw was a Jew. In addition, numerous refugees seeking protection from Nazi persecution in Germany and Austria found a haven in Poland. The first bombs of Hitler's air force were dropped on Warsaw. The city was bombed on 1 September 1939, and was threatened by Hitler's encircling armies only a few days later. Among the impressions I retain most vividly of those difficult days in Warsaw are the selflessness and dedication with which the Jews — including Orthodox members of the community, who usually lived in complete isolation from their Polish surroundings — helped us erect barricades and took part in the battle. After the siege, which lasted several weeks, Warsaw — one of the last parts of the country still offering resistance — had to surrender. This marked the beginning of the tragic years of the occupation, which would, as everyone knew, be fraught with great hardships for the Poles. The large number of Jews in occupied Poland posed a problem. The attempt to save them cannot be examined without knowing the conditions under which the Polish people were living. These conditions were different from and considerably harsher than, for example, those experienced by the French, the Belgians, the Dutch, or the Danes. Along with the Jews, it was only the peoples of the occupied countries of Eastern Europe who would have been completely wiped out had Hitler been victorious. During the Nuremberg Trials, Himmler's so-called *Generalplan Ost* [the overall plan the Germans had formulated for the occupied territories to the east of Germany after final victory — ED.] became public knowledge. According to this plan, fifty million Slavs, among them about twenty million Poles, were to have been forcibly resettled to Siberia after the German victory over the Soviet Union, and the Polish intelligentsia was to be totally annihilated.

The Nazis carried out their step-by-step plan for the extermination of the Jews in Poland so perfectly that neither the Jewish community nor their Christian sym-

pathizers were completely aware of the terrible situation
or of the Nazis' final designs until the end of 1941.

The binding regulations concerning the conduct of
Christian Poles toward the Jews in the occupied areas
of Poland had already been drawn up in Berlin on 21
September 1939, in other words, prior to the conclusion
of the campaign in Poland. The head of the *Reichssicherheitshauptamt* (RSHA, the National Central Security Office), Reinhard Heydrich, recommended that the
leaders of the *Einsatzgruppen* (combat groups) of the
Security Police distinguish between "the final goal,
which will require more time, and individual phases
leading up to the final goal, which will be achieved more
quickly." In so doing, he emphasized that "all of the
planned steps, and thus the final goal as well, are to be
treated as strictly confidential and secret."

The first phase was to isolate the entire Jewish population in certain cities and at the same time to install
local Councils of Elders invested with "the complete
responsibility . . . for the precise and timely execution
of issued directives." On 30 October 1939 an order from
Himmler decreed that all Jews from Pomerania and the
provinces of Poznań and Upper Silesia relocate to the
so-called *General Gouvernement*,[2] which had been established in an area in central Poland, within four
months, together with a sizable number "of the especially hostile Polish population."

The plan was carried out with the utmost ruthlessness.
Several thousand people, Christians and Jews alike, were
transported in unheated stockcars without the slightest
provisions during the winter months of 1939/40, mainly
into the province of Lublin, Kraków, and Kielce. There
were many deaths along the way.

In the meantime, more and more detailed directives
concerning the Jews were being issued in the *General*

Gouvernement. The occupation forces charged the newly created Jewish Councils with the responsibility of providing for the subsistence of the Jewish population, without, however, guaranteeing them the means to do so. Those classified as Jews had their choice of where to live and their freedom of movement restricted by the legislation of the occupying administration. In practical terms, property rights were also greatly restricted. Jews were obliged to wear a white armband with a blue star. One of the cruelest directives for people between the ages of fourteen and sixty was forced labor — a directive that was implemented in an especially ruthless manner. The Germans organized the first forced labor camps for the Jews at the beginning of 1940. In its issue of 9 January 1941, the *Biuletyn Informacyjny* ["Information Bulletin"], the publication of the underground Union for Armed Resistance [*Zwiazek Walki Zbrojnej* — ZWZ], reported:

What we know about the camps for Jews that have been in existence since the spring of last year is horrifying.

A Jewish camp is actually no different from Auschwitz. People who are not at all conditioned to work in the fields in winter, who lack appropriate clothing, and who are pathetically undernourished, are driven from their farms and villages and housed in unheated sheds and barracks. The treatment is sadistic! The mortality rate is incredible!

At the same time, there were reports of the execution of many hundreds of Christian Poles in Poznań, Bydgoszcz, and in the area around Warsaw. Tens of thousands of intellectuals, including scientists (among them professors from Jagiellonian University in Kraków), teachers, lawyers, priests, government officials, and functionaries of the political parties, were being transported to the concentration camps in Sachsenhausen, Dachau, and the recently established camp at Auschwitz. All of these developments made it difficult to realize what the Nazis' actual plans for the Jews were during the first months of the occupation. It was the creation of the ghettos, which took place in the larger cities of central Poland during the fall of 1940 and at the beginning of 1941, that finally aroused tremendous concern.

In Łódź — which had the second largest Jewish population in Poland — a ghetto had been created during the first months of 1940 in accordance with the directive of 8 February 1940. This ghetto, conceived as a temporary area of isolation, was in reality a large forced labor camp. More than 160,000 people were crammed together in an area of approximately four square kilometers, which meant there was an average of six persons to a room. Almost all of them — including children as young as ten — worked in industrial plants, generating enormous profits for hundreds of German companies. Eventually, able-bodied Jews from Brest in Kujawia, Belchatow, Wieluń, Sieradz, Zgierz, Brzeziny, Pabianice, and many other towns were settled in the Łódź ghetto. In the fall of 1941 approximately 20,000 Jews arrived who had been deported from Vienna, Berlin, Frankfurt am Main, Dusseldorf, Cologne, Emden, Luxembourg, and Prague.

In the *General Gouvernement* the first ghetto was created in Piotrków as early as October of 1939. In the two cities with the largest Jewish populations, however, ghettos were not established until much later: in Warsaw in November of 1940 and in Kraków not until March of 1941. Initially, approximately 400,000 people had been crammed within the boundaries of the high-walled Jewish section of Warsaw. The living conditions in the ghettos soon proved unbearable. The *Biuletyn Infor-*

macyjny devoted its lead article on 23 May 1941 to a description and analysis of these conditions:

The sequestration of the Jews has had many consequences, especially economic ones. Those living in the ghetto have been compelled to trade exclusively with fellow Jews, the majority of whom are not wealthy; indeed, the great majority are absolutely without resources. Being cut off from the outside world has made it impossible to import food and has made smuggling it in considerably more difficult. This is accelerating the spreading misery. Forcing the Jews together in what was already the worst section of the city had dire consequences for their health. As an example we will list some details from the Warsaw ghetto: The ghetto was established in an unusually densely settled section of the city. It was sited in such a manner that it does not have a park and does not border on the Vistula River; the only green area is the cemetery. The population density is unimaginable. An average of six people live in one room; sometimes, however, there are as many as twenty. According to information from the census bureau, there are seventy people per hectare in greater Warsaw; in contrast, in the ghetto there are 1,110.

Being cut off from the surrounding world deprives a substantial number of the Jews of their income. Within the ghetto, hardly 10 percent to 20 percent are employed in stores or workshops. . . . In addition, the possessions of the Jews are vanishing to the outside because of smuggling. The ghetto, having been restricted to internal trade, is selling itself, for this is the only way it can obtain the money to survive. As a consequence of the lack of goods and raw materials, old reserves are increasingly being used up. This exhaustion of resources is causing ever increasing poverty. In the ghetto, the prices of industrial goods are not much higher than they were before the war, while the price of food, already terribly high throughout Warsaw, is much higher in the ghetto. Consider that Jews can obtain bread only with ration cards, that they are limited to 750 grams a week, and add to that the complete lack of fuel during the winter — then we can imagine the dreadful fate of these people.

The transportation of Jews from the cities and towns of the district of Warsaw into the already overcrowded and starved Warsaw ghetto began in January. The population of the ghetto increased to 500,000. This increased crowding resulted in unspeakable hygienic and sanitary conditions. Hunger and unimaginable misery are now prevalent. Sluggish groups of pale, emaciated people slink through the overcrowded streets; there are beggars sitting and lying along the walls; the sight of someone collapsing from starvation is not rare. The home for foundlings receives more than ten infants daily, and several people die on the streets every day. Contagious diseases, above all tuberculosis, are spreading.

At the same time, the plundering of wealthy Jews by the Germans has not stopped. Their treatment of Jews was and remains inhuman. Abuses — wild, bestial "amusements" — are daily events.

Mortality, especially among children and the aged, increased more than tenfold in comparison to the death rate before the war. In Łódź, for example, the number of people who died of natural causes in 1942 was 159.8 per 1,000 Jewish inhabitants, while before the war the number had never risen above 9.6 per 1,000; in Lublin, 47.5 per 1,000 Jews died in 1941 in comparison to the prewar figures of 12.6 per 1,000. These grim physical statistics grew increasingly starker.

Given these circumstances, many Poles faced the moral necessity of helping those Jews, who, to avoid being forced into ghettos, decided to go into hiding. However, only a few Jews, mainly from intellectual or artistic circles, decided to risk an illegal existence with forged papers bearing "Aryan" names.

Obviously, for most of these people their attachment to their surroundings and their families, as well as the economic conditions, were inhibiting factors. They gave in to the illusion that an Allied victory was not far off and that their forced stay in the ghettos would not last long.

But in the course of time attempts at escape from the ghetto became more frequent. The number of Jews whom the Christian population helped to hide increased considerably. Obviously aware of this fact, the Nazis retaliated. A directive from Hans Frank of 15 October 1941 states:

Jews who leave their designated area of residence without authorization will be executed. The same applies to persons who knowingly grant shelter to such Jews. . . . Instigators and accessories will be punished in the same manner as the perpetrators; the attempt will be treated like the completed act.

Selling or giving food to a Jew — even giving a glass of water to someone dying of thirst — was considered to be aiding a Jew. Under such conditions, any attempt to help the persecuted brought with it the danger of having one's entire family annihilated, as the Nazis generally invoked the principle of collective guilt in such cases. This was already true before the mass genocide began.

During the last months of 1941 and at the beginning of 1942, reports of mass executions of Jews arrived in Warsaw, Kraków, and other centers of the Polish resistance in the interior of the country. They originated in the German-occupied areas during the first months following the outbreak of war with the Soviet Union on 22 June 1941. There was talk of mass executions in the area of Białystok, in Vilnius, in the city and province of

Novogrudok, in Polesie and Wołyń, in Lvov and its province, as well as in Stanisławów and Ternopol.

In December of 1941, the extermination camp in Chełmno on the Ner River, where men, women, and children from the small cities of the Warta district and the ghetto in Łódź were sent to their deaths, was "made operational." These reports were repeated by the Polish underground press, but the majority of Jews did not believe them. As is normal in situations of stress and isolation, Jews and Christian Poles detained in prisons and camps yielded to the hope of effective intervention by the Allies and of a quick end to the war. One of the youth functionaries of the "Bund" [a Jewish socialist organization — ED.] in the Warsaw ghetto, Marek Edelman, noted the following in 1945:

The Warsaw ghetto did not believe this information. These people could not believe that the life they were so attached to could be taken from them in such a manner. Only the organized youth, watchfully observing the gradual increase of German terror, recognized the reality and decided to initiate a broad information campaign for the population.

The decision on the "final solution to the Jewish question" was made in Berlin on 20 January 1942. The minutes of the meeting that took place under the supervision of the head of the *Reichssicherheitshauptamt* contain the following:

If approved by the Führer, another possible solution would be the evacuation of the Jews to the East instead of emigration. This should, however, only be considered as a secondary possibility; it would, however, add to the accumulated experience that will be necessary for the future final solution to the Jewish question.

During the final solution to the European Jewish question about 11 million Jews need to be considered. . . . The practical execution of the final solution will comb Europe from West to East. . . .

Secretary of State Dr. Bühler noted that the *General Gouvernement* would welcome the final solution being initiated there, as transportation and work-related problems would not be of overriding importance nor would they disrupt the course of the action. The Jews must be removed from the area of the *General Gouvernement* as quickly as possible. . . .

No one could imagine the possibility of the completely senseless killing of thousands of innocent men, women, and children. During 1942, however, the last remnants of any illusions were lost; the Germans initiated the complete liquidation of the ghettos in various parts of Poland by sending their inhabitants to the newly created extermination camps in Treblinka, Sobibor, Belzec, Auschwitz-Birkenau, and Majdanek under the pretext of resettlement.

The resettlement of the Jewish population in the area of Lublin and in the small cities around Warsaw started in March of 1942. The methods used were the same everywhere: the Nazis shot the sick and the feeble in their homes, in hospitals, and asylums, as well as the children in orphanages; the able-bodied were driven to the transporters with unusual brutality.

As Marek Edelman wrote in 1945:

Lacking direct contact with the countryside, the Warsaw ghetto views these reports with suspicion and lists thousands of arguments to destroy even the remotest chance of their probability. The idea that a similar crime could be repeated in the capital of Poland, where more than 300,000 Jews live, is unthinkable.

During the night of 17/18 April 1942 the Gestapo organized a mass execution in the ghetto: fifty-two men, among them respected functionaries, were taken out of their homes and shot on the street.

The next day the whole ghetto is dismayed, numbed, enraged, speculates about the reasons for these executions. Since it was editors of illegal newspapers who were executed, the majority believes that the whole action is targeted at political functionaries, that political activities must stop to prevent an unnecessary increase in the already large number of victims. (Edelman)

On 30 April 1942 the *Biuletyn Informacyjny* published a lead article entitled "The Jews." Among other things, it discussed the conditions reigning in the Warsaw ghetto:

There are a number of so-called "special" houses where the poorest of the poor live, where death reaps too great a harvest. For example: in the house at 46 Mila Street, presently inhabited by 500 people, 233 people have died so far; in the house at 51 Mila Street, inhabited by 578 people, 250 died. In the house at 63 Pawia Street, inhabited by 794 people, 430 died, 200 of them during the last three months. The record in these wretched statistics is held by the house at 21 Krochmalna Street, inhabited by 400 people, where the same number of people died. The total extinction of whole families is a frequent occurrence in these "special" houses: in the house at 56 Zamenhoffa Street, ten families have literally died out; at 51 Mila Street, fifteen families; at 46 Mila Street, twenty-eight families. In many homes there is a complete lack of fuel. In seventeen "special" houses 710 out of approximately 780 rooms had no heat at all this winter. Whole families have frozen to death. The prevalence of disease is also incredible. For example, in the house at 63 Pawia Street, 750 of 794 inhabitants are sick, at 7 Ostrowska Street it is 252 of 287 inhabitants, at 14 Ostrowska Street it is 199 of 199 inhabitants, or literally all of the inhabitants.

In the house on Krochmalna Street the conditions are as follows: during the last three months 126 people died, 64 of typhus, the remainder of starvation. Sixty-three bodies were dumped on the street because there was no money for a decent burial. Three hundred sixty-five people contracted typhus. Nearly 100 people display tumors and nutritional edemas. During the last few months forty-five families were displaced; they were predominantly lodged in cellars without flooring, without windows, etc. At the moment there are twenty-eight families (140 people) who own absolutely nothing. These people live on bare floors, covered with rags, and subsist on raw vegetable garbage. . . .

The Germans are working to make these already horrible conditions even worse. Thus they are continuously decreasing the territory of the ghetto, while further increasing the resettlements of the Jews from the towns surrounding Warsaw (Okuniew, Zielonka, Rembertow, Milosna, Wawer) into the ghetto.

1 May 1942. A Nazi camera crew visits the Warsaw ghetto to take pictures to be used as propaganda.

3 May 1942. From the diary of the engineer Adam Czerniakow, the president of the Jewish Council in the ghetto:

Public office hours. The cameramen from Propaganda entered at 10 o'clock. They shot some film in my office. They staged the comings and goings of petitioners, rabbis, etc. Following that everything was removed from the walls. A nine-branched candelabrum was placed on my desk, its candles lighted. . . . The Transfer Office demanded a list of the ghetto administration employees, including the officials of the community council. Apparently there will be a transfer of unproductive elements from Warsaw.

On 12 May 1942 the Nazi film crew working in the ghetto demanded to film in the *mikvah* (the ritual baths) on Dzielna Street. "Two orthodox men with *peies* [sidelocks] and twenty upper-class women necessary for this. In addition, demonstration of a circumcision," Adam Czerniakow noted.

On 27 May 1942, 600 Jews forcibly relocated from Radzymin near Warsaw arrive in the Warsaw ghetto.

On 29/30 May 1942 the German police kill ten people at night in their homes in the Warsaw ghetto. The reason is not known. During the same night, 914 men, among them 150 juveniles between the ages of fifteen and nineteen, are removed from the ghetto to an unknown location.

On 10/11 June 1942 a number of known smugglers were murdered in the ghetto during the night. "Obviously," Dr. Emanuel Ringelblum remarked in his notebook on life in the ghetto,

the intent is to liquidate smuggling at any price through massacres and massive intimidation. Last night a number of smugglers were liquidated in the usual way. They were dragged out of their apartments and shot on the street. There was another massacre toward morning and yet another yesterday evening at the ghetto wall. . . . They are taking place all over, but mainly in the small ghetto on Krochmalna and Ciepla streets.

On 2 July 1942, between four and six in the morning, 110 people were removed from the ghetto and executed. Among them were ten women and ten members of the *Jüdischer Ordnungsdienst,* the Jewish ghetto police. A notification with Auerswald's signature announced this event publicly. The underground publication of the socialist "Bund" in the ghetto, the *Szturm* of 5 July, wrote the following:

Auerswald, the master henchman, has announced that 110 Jews were murdered for inciting insurrection, for resisting the Germans. Just let the henchman be aware of the fact that as of today we will no longer submit to Nazi law. We are not afraid of punishment, for we have nothing left to lose, but everything to win. Auerswald's notification is an honor to the fighting Jewish masses of the fighting ghetto.

In mid July of 1942 "the black cloud grew denser," Marek Edelman remembers.

Outwardly everything looks normal. There are some unlikely rumors circulating about the arrival of a resettlement detachment; that 20, 40 or 60 thousand inhabitants will be removed from the ghetto; that the unemployed will be forced to work on fortification systems; that only those working in Warsaw will remain there. These rumors cause alarm, sometimes panic, even though they are considered to be "improbable." People are literally stampeding to find work in factories, in social service institutions, in offices. Ladies who until now have been sitting in the coffee houses, are now turning into overworked seamstresses, menders, and civil servants with a vengeance. Some factories only employ people with their own sewing machine. The price for sewing machines increased immediately. People are ever more willing, ever more eager to pay more and more to obtain a job in a workshop. They talk about nothing else, they think about nothing else. Everyone has to work! Those "well situated," the lucky ones, breathe a sigh of relief, the "nonsituated," the anxious, the harried, desperately grasp at the slightest chance of work.

On 20 July 1942 Adam Czerniakow wrote the following:

At the Gestapo office at 7:30 A.M. I asked Mende how much truth there is to these rumors. He replied that he had not heard anything about it. I then turned to Brandt; he answered that he knew nothing. Asked whether something like this could happen, he responded that he knew nothing. Uncertain, I walked away from him. I turned to his boss, Inspector Boehm. He replied that it was not his business, that Mehenmann might be able to comment on the rumors. I remarked that, according to what was being said, resettlement was to begin this evening at 7:30. His answer was that he would certainly know something if it were to start today. Lacking any other recourse, I went to the deputy of the head of Section III, Scherer. He expressed amazement about the rumors and stated that there was nothing to be afraid of. He answered that I could announce that everything that was being said was nonsensical and ridiculous. I ordered Lejkin (he was the commander of the Jewish Police in the Warsaw ghetto) to inform the population of this via the districts.

21 July 1942:
"Things started to develop with great speed," Adolf and Barbara Berman noted in *The Destruction of the Jewish Ghetto in Warsaw*, a chronicle they wrote after "crossing over" to the "Aryan" sector of Warsaw in October of 1942.

The Gestapo arrested a number of aldermen and took them to the *pawiak*. Additional people were apprehended on the streets and taken to the *pawiak* as hostages. Everything was dominated by a feeling of unusual oppression and anxiety. It was assumed that the arrests meant that the Jewish Council was being dissolved and that this was the beginning of the liquidation of the ghetto. This assumption about the Jewish

Council proved to be unfounded, as the arrest of the council members was a coercive move to intensify the sense of panic and simultaneously to acquire a certain number of hostages. Some of the council members were released after a day or two; most of these managed the supply office (Gepner, Sztolcman, Kobryner, and others). Czerniakow, the president, had not been arrested although the rumor was also circulating. Dr. Wielikowski, the head of social services, was released immediately following his arrest.

Dr. Franciszek Raszeja, a professor at Poznań University and the medical director of the surgical department of the Warsaw PCK (the Polish Red Cross) hospital, was shot in the home of his patient, Abe Gutnajer, on Chlodna Street. "He had been called to the patient and was in possession of a valid permit," Professor Ludwik Hirzfeld remembers. "His former assistant Dr. Kazimierz Polak, a nurse, and some relatives were present. The gentlemen from the SS broke into the apartment and murdered everyone."

On 21 July 1942 Janusz Korczak (Henryk Goldszmit) wrote:

Tomorrow I will be sixty-three or sixty-four years old. My father did not keep a family journal for several years. This has created some difficult situations for me. Mother called it culpable negligence: as a lawyer, he (father) should not have let the matter of the family journal slide.

I was named after my grandfather. His name was Hersz (Hirsz). My father was entitled to call me Henryk; he himself was given the name Jozef. Grandfather gave the other children Christian names: Maria, Magdalena, Ludwik, Jakub, Karol.

I should dedicate much space to my father, as I gradually realize what he strove for, what grandfather, wearing himself out, strove for for so many years.

And mother. Some later time. I am mother as well as father. I know this, and thanks to this I understand much. Great-grandfather was a glazier. This makes me glad: glass gives off warmth and light. It is a difficult thing, to be born and to learn to live. What remains for me is a much easier task: to die. After death it may be difficult again, but I do not think about that. The last year, or month, or hour.

I want to be conscious and cognizant. I do not know what I would say to the children as a farewell. I would want to say so much, including that they have complete freedom to choose their path in life. Ten o'clock. Shots: two, several, two, one, several. Perhaps my window is poorly darkened right now. But I will not interrupt my writing. The opposite: my thoughts take flight (a single shot).

On 22 July 1942 SS *Hauptsturmführer* Hoefle entered the building of the Jewish community at 26 Gryzbowska Street at 10 A.M. with his attendants. Czerniakow was told that — with a few exceptions — the Jews were to be moved to the East without regard to gender or age. By that afternoon at four, 6,000 people were to be ready. And this would be the minimum each day.

That day the following directive was posted in the ghetto on Hoefle's orders (Czerniakow had not signed it at the time):

Jewish Council in Warsaw
Warsaw, 22 July 1942

NOTICE

1. By order of the German authorities all Jews living in Warsaw will be resettled to the East, regardless of age and gender.

2. The following are not affected:

(a) all Jewish persons who are working in German offices or institutions and who can supply proof thereof;

(b) all Jewish persons who are members of the Jewish Council or who are employees of the Jewish Council (the cutoff date is the day of the publication of this directive);

(c) all Jewish persons working for German companies and who can supply proof thereof;

(d) all able-bodied Jewish persons who are not yet integrated into the work force; these are to be interned in the Jewish district;

(e) all Jewish persons on the staffs of the Jewish hospitals. The same applies to the members of the Jewish disinfection teams;

(f) all Jewish persons belonging to the Jewish Police;

(g) all Jewish persons who are direct family members of persons listed in (a) – (f). Only wives and children are considered to be family members;

(h) all Jewish persons who are in a Jewish hospital on the first day of resettlement and who cannot be discharged. Their suitability for discharge will be determined by a physician selected by the Jewish Council.

3. Each Jewish person being resettled is permitted to take along 15 kilograms of personal belongings. All valuables — gold, jewelry, money, etc. — can be taken along. A three-day supply of food must be packed.

4. Resettlement will begin on 7/22/1942 at 11 A.M.

5. Penalties:

(a) all Jewish persons leaving the ghetto as of the beginning of the resettlement who are not among the people listed in (2a) and (2c), inasmuch as they have not been entitled to do so thus far, will be shot;

(b) all Jewish persons engaging in actions to disrupt or avoid the resettlement program will be shot;

(c) all Jewish persons supporting action to disrupt or avoid the resettlement program will be shot;

(d) all Jews found in Warsaw after the conclusion of the resettlement who do not belong to the group of people listed in (2a) – (2h) will be shot.

Warsaw Jewish Council

In his chronicle (written on the basis of eyewitness reports by Christian Poles who had been permitted to live in the ghetto and published by the underground *Geheime Militärische Verlagsanstalt* [Secret Military Publishing Institute] under the title "The Liquidation of the Warsaw Ghetto" in October of 1942) Antoni Szymanowski, an officer in the *Armia Krajowa* — the so-called Polish Home Army — noted the following:

Wednesday, 7/22/1942. So this is the end of the ghetto that has been fighting desperately to stay alive for two years. This afternoon it was announced that everyone, regardless of sex or age, will be resettled "to the East." There is no need to fool ourselves; the announcement is a death sentence. The Germans will not settle, feed, and clothe thousands of people in any "East" after consistently exterminating them in Warsaw. Death — whether sudden or gradual — is waiting for them. Perhaps those exempted from resettlement have a chance to survive since they are useful to the Germans: the ones working for them in factories and in the trades, the police, the city employees, etc. They are even permitted to protect their wives and children from being deported. But the rest? Do we need any more indication than that amazingly cynical sentence: each person being resettled is permitted to take along fifteen kilograms of his personal belongings. All valuables such as money, jewelry, gold can be taken along. Gold, which Jews have been forbidden to own for months now! Line up in rows so that we can kill you, but have your jewelry ready to save us trouble!

... The Jewish Police have been hunting for humans since noon. The Germans are staying out of it. There are two kinds of them: black and red, according to their uniforms. Machine guns have been posted at all city egresses, and bursts of fire can be heard almost continously, but they seem to be more of a deterrent. But the wild, even frenzied shooting has been going on all night. They are shooting into windows with carbines, at passersby with revolvers. Today a doctor from the hospital on Sienna Street told me that there is not a room left in her building that has not been shot into from the street. ...

Larger groups are led to the connection track in the square on Stawki Street. Our messenger ran over there and caught a glimpse of how they were hastily loaded into open railway cars; when a car was full, it was wired shut with barbed wire, worse than with animals! It is raining, and the sight of this agony is — he says — unbearable. ... The atmosphere of panic and terror, intensified by the continuous reverberations of erratic shooting, is so terrible that I breathed a sigh of relief when I left the ghetto in the evening. At the same time, though, it was difficult for me, after watching the more or less normal life on the streets of Warsaw, really to believe that this "re-settlement" of hundreds of people into the beyond is taking place right beside it.

On 23 July 1942 Adolf Berman reported the following:

The inhabitants of the remaining refugee quarters have been moved and the evacuation of the poorest from the city districts containing the so-called death houses — those that have the highest mortality rates — has begun. This is where the greatest number of orphans lived (many houses on Ostrowska, Pawia, Krochmalna streets, etc.). On the same day the children were also removed from the orphanage at 3 Dzika Street in spite of assurances (by the Jewish Police) that the orphanages would be left alone for the time being. This was explained by saying that the orphanage is considered a part of the refugee camp. Then the occupants of the so-called nursery at 6 Gesia Street were taken away too.

Because of the intervention of the Center for the Protection of Children (CENTOS) by the commander's office of the Jewish Police, the orphanages have been left alone. The situation remained this way up to the moment the Germans took over the process themselves. I went to see the wife of Czerniakow, the chairman, in connection with the resettlement of the children from the two houses; I wanted to ask her to use her influence as a member of the administration of CENTOS with her husband. I found her in a state of unusual depression; as she talked the tears were just streaming down her face. All I could get out of her was that the children's prospects do not look good. Her husband had told her he would kill himself if he had to sign the directive regarding the resettlement of the children.

The last sentence in the diary of Adam Czerniakow, from the entry dated 23 July 1942:

The response to the question of how many days a week the process was to take place was seven. In the city everyone is crowding to find work. A sewing machine can save lives. Three o'clock. So far, 4,000 have been moved out. According to the directives it is to be 9,000 by four o'clock. Some functionaries appeared at the post office and ordered that all arriving letters and packages be sent to the *pawiak*.

Less than an hour after writing these words, Adam Czerniakow took his own life.

The first removal of inhabitants of the Warsaw ghetto to Treblinka II took place the same day.

By 24 July 1942 it was clear that the resettlement process was systematically being expanded to all districts of the city. Raids, so-called blockades, were initiated for this purpose. "This morning we experienced the block-ading of the house at 29 Orgrodowa Street," Adolf and Barbara Berman wrote.

At about 6 A.M. we were awakened by an incredible noise: a large detachment of the ZSP [Jewish Police] appeared in the courtyard and surrounded the gate. After a while we heard loud orders: "All occupants of the house into the courtyard! People to be resettled may take along 15 kilograms of luggage. Persons exempted from resettlement must present their papers!" There was great confusion. Half-dressed people gathered in the yard, showed their identification papers and certificates. The police spread out into the stairways, attics, and cellars and started dragging the people who had hidden outside. Shortly thereafter some trucks drove into the yard. Those who had hidden were thrown onto the trucks. The others, those who had come down into the courtyard voluntarily, were lined up and their papers were examined. They were treated quite liberally and everyone who had any kind of documen-tation from a shop or a social institution was let go. Oral explanations or protestations, however, were in vain, as was outward appearance. The trucks contained able-bodied young men, clean and well dressed. Many of them did not live in the house; they were there because a shop was to be set up in it. They had moved machines into the house and had counted on receiving some type of temporary certificate that would exempt them from resettlement for a while. Four trucks full of people, about 120, were taken away. Feeling that they were not threatened for the moment, the remaining occu-pants — several hundred people lived here — immediately started to organize help for those being taken away. The rep-resentatives of the Citizens' Committee gave money to the peo-ple on the trucks, 20 and 50 zlotys each. Those remaining in the house were asked to share their bread, for the people in the trucks were crying out that they were hungry, and it was probably impossible to obtain bread for any amount of money at the collection point. Especially heartrending scenes took place when families were torn apart. The notification did state that an employee could exempt his closest relatives, i.e., wife and children, from resettlement, but after a few days it became apparent that that, too, was a deception. In reality neither parents nor siblings were spared — with the exception of the families of police officers. Consequently there were many cases in which people who were exempt from resettlement and who had relaxed about their fate were once again thrown into desperation as their fathers, mothers, brothers, sisters were dragged onto the trucks.

From the diary entries of the teacher and historian Abraham Lewin:

It rains all day. Everyone is crying. The Jews are crying. They believe in a miracle. The resettlement continues. The blockades of the tenements . . . 23 Twarda Street. Stirring images . . . six in the morning. Activity on the streets like during the bombardment of Warsaw. The Jews are running through the streets as though possessed, dragging along children and carrying bales of linens. The Germans have surrounded the tenement on Karmelicka-Nowolipie Street. Mothers and children are wandering about the streets like lost sheep. Where is my child? Lamentation!

Another dreary day. It is raining. Scenes that took place in the house at 25 Nowolipie Street. A big street raid. Old men and women, children, boys and girls, are hauled off. They are seized by police officers and officials from the Community Council. The latter wear white armbands on their forearms. They help the police. . . . How do the Jews try to save themselves? Fictitious marriages with police officers. Gutta married the brother of her husband.

During the raids the police act like wild animals. Their cruelties: they drag girls off of bicycles, empty out apartments, let possessions fall prey to the flames. Incomparable pogroms and killings. . . . Great hunger in the Warsaw ghetto. Someone saved his sister with her four-year-old daughter by passing her off as his wife. The child did not reveal the secret, she called out: Papa! I am trying to save my father with the aid of a certificate from the Jewish Social Cooperative.

On 24 July 1942 a notice was posted on orders of the German police. It was intended to calm public opinion and was signed by the Jewish Council:

NOTICE

1. Because of incorrect information circulating in the Jewish quarter of Warsaw in connection with the resettlement program, the Warsaw Jewish Council has been empowered by the administrative authorities to announce that the resettlement of the unproductive population in the Jewish quarter of Warsaw is really to the East.

2. In the interest of the population the resettlement should take place within the established time frame. The Warsaw Jewish Council calls on everyone subject to resettlement not to hinder or avoid resettlement, as this will only complicate the execution of the program.

3. As is generally understood by most of the Jewish inhabitants of Warsaw, it is appropriate that persons being resettled, who live in sequentially designated houses, report voluntarily to the assembly point at 6/8 Stawki Street.

In accordance with the promise we have received, families reporting voluntarily will not be separated.

Warsaw, 24 July 1942

Warsaw Jewish Council

On 27 July 1942 Antoni Szymanowski wrote:

Today I heard of the death of the well-known painter K[ramsztyk]. While he was being removed from his apartment he did not walk down the stairs quickly enough, so the German simply shot him in the back of the head. In the ghetto everything is based on the principle of moving quickly — even into one's own death. The word "quick" means "run."

During the last days of July a conference of social and political functionaries was held in the assembly room of the ZTOS (the Jewish Society for Social Welfare) at 25 Nowolipki Street. The topic was a discussion of the situation in the ghetto. Prominent representatives of various groups and organizations were present, from the orthodox religious party Agudat to the communist PPR/Polish Workers Party. Heinz Berliński, a member of the underground movement in the Warsaw ghetto and later a cofounder of the Jewish Combat Organization, noted the following in his April 1944 report:

The participants in the conference were impressed by the comments made by Zysie Frydman and Schiper. Frydman said: "I believe in God, I believe there will be a miracle. God will not permit the extermination of the Jewish people. To fight the Germans is absolutely senseless. The Germans can liquidate us all within a few days. And if we do not fight, the ghetto will last longer, and then perhaps the miracle will occur. Those among my friends who trust in the Allies should not despair, for they believe in an Allied victory. Or do they doubt that the Allies will bring them freedom? And those among my friends who believe in the revolution and the Soviet Union are convinced that only the Red Army will bring freedom. Thus they should continue to believe in the Red Army. Dear friends, if we remain steadfast and retain our faith, we will live to see our liberation!"

Schiper spoke out against self-defense. "Self-defense means the destruction of the whole Warsaw ghetto! I believe we will succeed in saving a certain percentage of the ghetto's inhabitants. It is war, and everyone has to make sacrifices. So we, too, have to sacrifice to save a certain number of people. If I were convinced that we will not succeed in this, my train of thoughts would be a different one!"

The participants in the conference separated with the intention of meeting again. The course of events, however, made it impossible to hold such deliberations a second time.

On 28 and 29 July, Adolf Berman reported:

The Germans initiated systematic blockades — simultaneously with the blockades carried out by the ZSP [Jewish Police] — together with Ukrainian units and Lithuanian infantry [i.e., members of Lithuanian fascist units associated with the Nazis]. They were unusually brutal and were generally not directed at individual houses; rather, they encompassed whole blocks and streets. The blockades started with intensive shooting, during which they killed people looking out of windows and balconies, as well as those who tried to hide. After that came the order: "Everyone out!" The Ukrainians spread out in the stairways and apartments and herded the inhabitants of the houses into the yard with their rifle butts, where they were ordered to line up. Initially, the Germans examined their papers, accepting some of them, for example physicians, dentists, and employees of the community and their families. The examination was quite cursory; the result of the examination always depended on the mood of the Germans; a relatively small percentage was let go. Surrounded by a cordon of Ukrainians, the large number of those remaining was forced to the "transportation point" in marching columns of rows of five. On the way, they shot those who tried to flee, who talked to someone, or who broke ranks. Pedestrians on the street were also shot at. Thus everyone hid in hallways as long as the "excursion" lasted, the streets were swept clean, the Germans blockaded the houses that usually had already been subjected to a blockade by the Jewish Police. In the process they arrested the people who had been passed over earlier and thus felt completely safe, so that they immediately came down into the courtyard when told to by the Germans. During the German blockades the orphanages were generally not spared either. Their first victim was the orphanage at 29 Ogrodowa Street.

On 28 July 1942 the Zionist-socialist Jewish Combat Organization (JCO) was founded in the Warsaw ghetto. Szmul Breslaw, Jitzchak Cukierman, Cywia Lubetkin, Jozef Kapłan, and Mordechai Tenenbaum were members of its command staff. With the goal of forging closer ties to the Polish underground and of receiving military support, liaison personnel from the ghetto, both men and women, were sent out, among them Arie Wilner ("Jurek"). Parallel to the newly created Combat Organization, groups of the "Bund" — cells of the PPR (Polish Workers Party) — not under the JCO's command were active in the ghetto, as was the Jewish Military Association (ZZW). This group was created out of the former Jewish Combat Organization by a group of officers and noncommissioned officers of the Polish Army Reserve as well as by members of the rightist, Zionist organization Betar.

On 29 July the following proclamation was posted in the ghetto. It was signed by the "Head of Police," who at that time was Jozef Szcrynski.

In accordance with the directives of the administrative authorities, I am informing those to be resettled that every person who voluntarily reports for resettlement on the 29th, 30th, and 31st of July of this year will be given provisions, i.e., 3 kilograms of bread and 1 kilogram of marmelade. Stawki Square at the corner of Dzika Street will be the assembly and food distribution point.

This proclamation was repeated on 1 August. In addition to the food, a promise was given not to separate families that reported voluntarily. "That is sufficient," Marek Edelman wrote.

Propaganda and hunger do the rest. The propaganda supplies an irrefutable argument against all the "fairy tales" about gas chambers: "Why should they share their bread if they intended to kill us!" The motivation of hunger is even stronger — it veils everything with the thought of three brown, freshly baked loaves of bread. Their taste is almost tangible, since all that separates you from them is the short distance to the point from where the freight cars leave, it causes the eyes to stop seeing what awaits you there; their smell, so known, so good, stupefies, deludes thoughts, they cease to comprehend what seems so apparent. There are days when hundreds of people stay at the transportation point, when they wait in a row for days for their resettlement. There are so many people who want the 3 kilograms of bread that the trains, already leaving twice a day with 12,000 people each, are unable to hold them all.

These events had a relatively broad effect among the Christian Poles. The first reports were published by the underground press, with more detailed information given by the underground weekly journals. For example, the following was written in the central publication of the Home Army, the *Biuletyn Informacyjny* (number 30 of 30 July 1942):

For the last week the main event affecting the city has been the liquidation of the ghetto by the Germans. This is being carried out with total Prussian efficiency. . . . Accompanied by continuous terror and the killing of many people, the evacuation has gone on day after day since then. . . . The atmosphere in the ghetto is filled with fear. The streets are empty. No one can be seen in the windows. Since all but two of the entrances into the ghetto have been walled off and the searches have been greatly intensified, the smuggling of provisions has been halted. As the rations for the Jewish population consist only of bread anyway, and then only 70 grams a day, the price of food immediately increased astronomically. For example, one kilogram of bread costs 80 to 100 zlotys.

The ghetto is surrounded by an impermeable chain of police and a Lithuanian unit. During the past few days these forces have been reinforced by SS guards. . . . More than 6,000 Jews are deported every day. They are transported in railway cars starting at the track on Stawki Street. Destination: the East. The actual destination of those deported is unknown. Rumors indicate the area around Malkinia and Brest on the Bug River. Their fate is also not known. The most pessimistic assumptions are circulating about this. As for organizing the deportation, in their devilish inventiveness the Germans have passed this task on to the Jewish Council and the Jewish Police.

Subsequent editions of the *Biuletyn Informacyjny* gave further precise information about events in the ghetto. Similar information, frequently supported by eyewitness reports of Nazi atrocities, appeared in the underground publications of secret military, political, and social organizations, whether they were of a democratic, nationalist, socialist, or communist persuasion.

During the first days of August 1942, the underground Catholic social education organization Front for Reborn Poland published 5,000 copies of a leaflet entitled "Protest," written by the important Catholic author Zofia Kossak-Szatkowska. She appealed to the hearts and consciences of all devout Christian Poles, as well as to all those who had disliked the Jews, asking them to adopt a morally unambiguous stance toward these crimes:

The world looks at this crime, worse than anything history has experienced so far, and — remains silent. Millions of defenseless humans are slaughtered in the midst of a general, sinister silence. The henchmen are silent. They do not brag about their deeds. England and America do not raise their voices; even the influential international Jewish community, so sensitive in its reaction to any transgression against its people earlier, is silent. Poland, too, is silent. The Christian Poles, the political friends of the Jews, confine themselves to a few newspaper reports; the Polish enemies of the Jews express a lack of interest in this matter that is foreign to them. The dying Jews are surrounded by a host of Pilates who are washing their hands in innocence. . . . We do not want to be Pilates! Actively, we can do nothing against the German slaughter, we cannot help, can save no one — but we protest from the depth of the hearts of those who are gripped by compassion, indignation, and horror. God demands this protest from us, God, who does not permit killing. Our Christian conscience demands it. Every being who thinks of himself as human has a right to charity. The blood of the helpless cries to the heavens for revenge. Those who do not support us in this protest are not Catholic!

On 4 August 1942 Janusz Korczak wrote in his diary:

I watered the flowers, the poor plants of the orphanage, the plants of the Jewish orphanage. The burned earth breathed a sigh of relief.

The sentry watched me work. Did my peaceful work at 6 A.M. antagonize him or touch him?

He stands there and watches, his legs far apart.

. . . The newspapers I worked on are defunct, discontinued, bankrupt. The publisher took his own life; he was ruined. And this not because I am a Jew, but because I was born in the East.

It could be a meager consolation that the proud West is not doing any better, either. It could be, but it is not. I wish evil on no one. I can't do that. I don't know how to.

. . . I water flowers. My bald head in the window — such a nice target.

He has a rifle. Why does he stand there watching quietly? He has no orders.

Perhaps he was a teacher in a small town during his civilian life, or a notary, a street cleaner in Leipzig, a waiter in Cologne?

What would he do if I were to nod my head at him?

Give him a friendly wave?

Perhaps he does not even know that things are as they are. It could be that he just arrived yesterday from far away. . . .

On 5 August 1942 — as reported by Adolf Berman, "the children were driven from their temporary quarters during a gruesome blockade of a number of streets in the 'Small Ghetto'; the orphanage had to relocate three times, and together with many thousands of people the orphans were herded to the transportation point." Korczak had many opportunities to save himself and secretly leave the ghetto, but he chose not to. He did not leave the children. Nor did his closest associate of many years, Stefania Wilczynska. An eyewitness to the last moments of the Korczak orphanage prior to the children's deportation to the gas chambers of Treblinka, Nachum Remba, former secretary of the Jewish community in Warsaw, noted the following in his report (preserved and maintained in the secret archives of the Warsaw ghetto founded by Dr. Emanuel Ringelblum):

The human mass ran densely packed, driven on by whips. Suddenly, Mr. Sz. [Szmerling — the Jewish commander at the transportation point] ordered that the orphans be moved out. Korczak was at the head of the procession! No! I will never forget the sight. It was not a simple boarding of the freight cars — it was an organized silent protest against this barbarism. In contrast to the densely packed masses, going like lambs to the slaughter, a procession unlike any before now began. All of the children had formed ranks in rows of four, with Korczak at their head, his eyes lifted to the sky; holding two children by their small hands, he led the procession. The second unit was led by Stefania Wilczynska, the third by Broniatowska — her children had blue backpacks — the fourth unit was led by Szternfeld from the boarding school on Twarda Street. . . . Even the Police stood still and saluted. When the Germans saw Korczak, they asked: "Who is this man?"

Janusz Korczak's heroism in going to his death in Treblinka with the children he cared for and refused to abandon was already a legend a few days later.

On 6 August 1942 the *Biuletyn Informacyjny* (no. 31) noted the following in a report on how the liquidation of the ghetto was proceeding:

Even though there were approximately fifty cars available daily at the transportation point during the first week of the "program," presently there were many more because of the increased numbers of people being deported. One hundred to one hundred fifty people are loaded into one car, shoved in with rifle butts. Prior to loading, the selection of the victims takes place. The women are separated from the men, children are snatched away from their mothers and put in different cars.

On 13 August 1942 Antoni Szymanowski noted:

The few Jews I knew personally from before the war had for the most part been baptized. There were, after all, quite a few of them; and many were added during the period the ghetto existed. This urge to be baptized by the hundreds, if not thousands, deserves considerable attention — especially since it no longer guaranteed the Jews' security or improved their chances. The newly converted, almost all of them from the ranks of the intelligentsia, grouped themselves around the parish of All Saints. Today, all of the priests of the parish, including Prelate Godlewski, were ordered out of the ghetto. And in

"Aryan" Warsaw, the search for refugees continues. The result of hiding outside of the ghetto, of helping a Jew — a bullet in the head.

From 9 to 16 August 1942 a number of directives were issued, which successively reduced the territory of the ghetto and obliged all inhabitants to abandon a number of streets immediately — within a few hours. This was done as follows: first, the people were driven out of the so-called Small Ghetto, i.e., the southern part around Chlodna Street, where only the workers in the barracks of some German factories were allowed to remain. As of the middle of August it was forbidden, under penalty of immediate execution, to live in the area south of Leszno Street or even to be found there. The seat of the Jewish Community Council was relocated from 26 Grzybowska Street to the building of the former military prison at 19 Zamenhoffa Street.

On 13 August 1942 the following excerpt appeared in a lengthy article entitled "Behind the Ghetto Walls" in a polemical journal of the Home Army, the *Wiadomosci Polskie* (nos. 14–15):

The extermination of millions of people for purely racial reasons deeply characterizes the ideology that has produced these murders as its fiendish offspring and final consequence. So after 2,000 years of the triumphant progress of Christ's teachings about brotherly love, and after even longer periods during which all the religions of the world preached the commandment "Thou shalt not kill," a people is living in the heart of Europe that calls itself Christian and, in the name of Christianity, is supposedly fighting Bolshevist godlessness, while committing these atrocities. . . . Perhaps it is necessary to go back to the Dark Ages, or even back to the time of prehistoric cavemen, to find equally brutal qualities. The human language lacks any expressions for them!

On the morning of 16 August 1942 troops of the Warsaw Gestapo commanded by SS-*Untersturmführer* Brandt started to arrest those staff members of the Jewish Community Council and its affiliated branches who had thus far been spared. More than 700 people were taken to the transportation point.

On 17 August 1942 announcements were circulated in the ghetto that the leadership, officers, and functionaries of the ghetto police were being indicted by the Jewish underground for zealous complicity in the extermination program.

On 19 August 1942 the daily raids and deportations in the Warsaw ghetto stopped for a few days. In the meantime, Nazi troops undertook similar extermination actions in the remaining Jewish settlements outside of Warsaw, mainly on the road to Otwock.

On 21 August 1942 Israel Kanal of the nationalist-conservative Akiba group tried to assassinate the commander of the Jewish Police in the Warsaw ghetto, Jozef Szerynski, in his home at 10 Nowolipki Street. Szerynski was wounded.

On 25 August 1942 Abraham Lewin noted in his diary:

Today it is five weeks since the slaughtering of the Jews in Warsaw and its environs began. The "program" continues. Today the Germans and the Ukrainians raided the block that housed the Community Council, i.e., Zamenhoffa, Pawia, Gesia, and Lubecka streets.

On 31 August 1942 Leon Feiner, the chairman of the secret central committee of the "Bund" in Poland wrote to Szmul Zygielbojm, a functionary of the "Bund" and a member of the National Council in London:

Here and there there were signs of active resistance. Houses were barricaded. . . . Resistance naturally resulted in imme-

diate and complete elimination. They were, after all, only spo-
radic occurrences. So far there has been no massive active
resistance and there is none now. The reasons:

1. The illusions nurtured by the enemy.

2. The officials and members of the Council are not inter-
ested in offering resistance because it endangers them.

3. The collective Jewish responsibility in bringing about their
own extermination is a tragic dilemma.

4. The obvious lack of support from abroad.

5. The absence of hope for aid from outside the ghetto.

The enlightened members of the Jewish working class and
intelligentsia know they have to resist actively, regardless of
the fact that resistance on a large scale will not be successful
because of the atmosphere and situation that the Germans
have deliberately created in and around the ghetto. However,
the conservative Jewish elements have opposed the idea for
tear of the immediate bloody retaliation by the Germans and
thus of its catastrophic consequences for the whole population.

During the first days of September 1942 the daily
resettlement from the ghetto continued with unrelenting
force. The Nazis post new notifications intended to dis-
courage aid to refugees:

NOTICE

Concerning: Death penalty for aiding Jews who have left
the Jewish section without authorization.

Recently, many Jews have left the Jewish section assigned
to them without authorization. At present they are still in the
district of Warsaw.

According to the Third Decree of the *General Gouvernement*
on residential restrictions in the *General Gouvernement* of 10-
15 1941 (VBL GG, S595), Jews who leave their assigned section without authorization will be executed. The same punishment applies to all who knowingly hide such Jews. This not

only applies to providing a place to sleep and food, but also to any other form of assistance, for example transportation in a vehicle of any kind, purchasing Jewish valuables, etc. . . .

I herewith request the population of the district of Warsaw to immediately report any Jew who is residing outside a Jewish section without authorization to the nearest police station or constabulary office.

Those who have aided or are now aiding a Jew and report this to the nearest police department prior to 4 P.M. on 9-9-42 will NOT BE SUBJECTED TO LEGAL PERSECUTION.

Similarly, those who deliver valuables purchased from Jews to 20 Nika Street in Warsaw or the nearest police station or constabulary office prior to 4 P.M. on 9-9-42 will not be subjected to legal action.

Warsaw, 5 September 1942

> Chief of the SS and the Police,
> District of Warsaw

In addition to enacting repressive laws, the occupying forces attempted to influence the Christian Polish population through propaganda. Posters, leaflets, and articles published by the Nazi press in the Polish language accused the Jews of being economic parasites, smugglers, usurers, and carriers of typhus, thus threatening the health and life of the "Aryans." Finally, the Jews were blamed for the outbreak of the war.

The Polish underground press attempted systematically to counteract these Nazi lies. In response to new repressive laws it intensified its appeals to save the victims of Nazi viciousness at any price.

The socialist journal *WRN* stated in its issue of 28 September 1942:

The Germans have imposed the death penalty for helping the few Jews who have managed to escape from their tormentors. Every decent human will treat this threat with contempt, for helping someone in distress, saving a fellow human being menaced by extermination, is a duty far beyond the fear of the death penalty. It is the duty of every single Christian Pole to help the victims of German bestiality.

The Marxist journal for society and culture *Przełom* ("The Breakthrough"), edited by Władysław Bienkowski, made the following appeal in its first issue of September 1942:

For two months we have been witness to the massacre of the Jewish population of Warsaw. . . . The blood of innocent Jewish victims and the blood of all those who have been executed in camps and prisons has been spilled for the delusion of world conquest; the murder of the defenseless is, to them, a step toward the fulfillment of their historic mission. . . . We call on all Christian Poles to help the victims who still survive.

In mid September of 1942 the leadership of the Civilian Combat Association made the following statement in the *Rzeczpospolita Polska* (no. 16), in the *Biuletyn Informacyjny* (no. 37), and in various other underground newspapers:

Alongside the tragic decimation that the Polish people is suffering at the hands of its enemies, the monstrous and deliberate slaughter of the Jews has been going on in our country for nearly a year. This mass murder is unprecedented in the history of the world; all the cruelties of history pale in comparison. Infants, children, teenagers, adults, old people, cripples, the infirm, the healthy, men, women, Jewish Catholics, and Jews of the Jewish faith are killed without mercy, without any reason other than their being members of the Jewish people. They are poisoned with gas, buried alive, thrown onto the pavement from tall buildings, while simultaneously suffering the additional degradation of slowly languishing away, the hell of humiliation and torment, and cynical abuse by their henchmen before they die. More than one million have been killed so far, and the number is increasing day by day.

As the leadership of the Civilian Combat Association cannot actively prevent this, it protests against the crimes committed against the Jews in the name of the whole Polish population. All of Poland's political and social organizations are united in this protest. The responsibility for the Christian victims as well as for the Jewish victims rests with the executioners and their abettors.

In the meantime, the penultimate act of the tragedy was taking place between 6 and 12 September 1942. Marek Edelman writes:

On 6 September 1942 all surviving inhabitants of the ghetto are told to report to the area circumscribed by Gesia, Zamenhoffa, Lubecka, and Stawki streets. This is where the final registration is to take place. . . . The whole population of the ghetto gathers in the small square bounded by these streets: factory workers, officials of the Jewish Council and the health services, employees of hospitals, and the sick are taken directly to the transportation point. The Germans have permitted a certain number of employees in each Germany company and in the Jewish Council to remain. Those chosen are given numbers. Numbers mean life. The chances are slim, but that they exist at all is sufficient once again to upset human rationality, to concentrate all thoughts on one thing, that obtaining a number is all important. Some struggle for a number loudly, they prove their right to exist by screaming; others await the ruling with tearful resignation. The final selection takes place amid the greatest suspense. After two days, during which each hour feels like a whole year, those chosen are taken to the work places where they are barracked. The rest are driven to the transportation point by the Germans. The families of the police come last.

What now takes place at the transportation point, when all hope has vanished, cannot be expressed in even the most unfeeling words. The invalids who were brought over earlier from the small hospital lie abandoned in cold rooms. They void themselves where they are and are left to lie in a stinking ooze of urine and filth. Nurses look for their mothers and fathers amid this turmoil, and with glistening eyes they inject them with comforting, death-summoning morphine.

The hand of some merciful doctor administers cyanide dissolved in water into the inflamed mouths of one unknown, sick child after another. . . . Cyanide — now it is the most precious, irreplaceable treasure. Cyanide means a quiet death; it saves them from the freight cars.

On the whole, the "great liquidation" of the Warsaw ghetto was complete by 12 September 1942. In the process more than 310,000 men, women, and children were sent to their deaths, most of them to Treblinka II. Officially, there were now only about 35,000 people living in the considerably smaller ghetto who worked for the Germans in various factories. In fact, however, an equal number of people had hidden in the ghetto. At least 10,000 to 20,000 people had managed to cross over to and hide in the "Aryan" sector of Warsaw just before the beginning of the "great action" or while it was going on. Nearly 70,000 Jews still lived within the walls of the Warsaw ghetto, not including those who were hiding among the Christian Polish population. Because of the mounting Nazi terror and the general misery, individual acts of assistance by people of good will were not sufficient. A comprehensive aid program was urgently needed. While the Zionist underground organizations and the "Bund" managed to reach an agreement to oppose the enemy on the Jewish side, an accord was reached between several underground organizations on the Polish side to create a common, illegal institution to help the Jews during the summer and fall months of 1942. I had the opportunity to work with this organization — which was later called the Council for Aid to Jews (*Rada Pomocy Żydom*) — from the time of its first inception and was able to participate personally in establishing contact with representatives of the "Bund" and the Zionist organizations during the fall of 1942.

Early in the summer of 1941 I returned to Warsaw with several hundred other men who had been released from Auschwitz. I had been arrested in 1940 during the course of a large-scale operation directed against the intelligentsia of Warsaw and taken to the camp where I was detained as a political prisoner, with the "protective custody inmate" number 4427. At the time I was just nineteen years old. But I was soon to gather experiences bitter beyond anything I had known, even though this was a time when there were as yet no gas chambers and mass executions — only "normal" deaths from exhaustion brought about by excessive work, unimaginable hunger, and brutal beatings. Before my arrest I was an employee of the Polish Red Cross in occupied Warsaw. The problems of charity work and of aiding people who had suffered the ravages of war were thus not unknown to me. In the camp, where I saw and experienced the deepest human misery, I developed the conviction that helping the victims of Nazi terror was of the utmost importance.

Prior to my internment in Auschwitz there was no ghetto in my home town. The encirclement of a section of Warsaw with a wall three meters high and the forced resettlement of a half a million people behind it were the most significant changes I encountered there upon my return. In the Christian Polish community, on the

"Aryan" side of the wall, several thousand Jews, perhaps more than ten thousand, lived illegally. They needed birth certificates and certificates of baptism issued in "Aryan" names, forged work permits and identification papers, a roof over their heads, and often financial support as well. My first attempt to help those living underground (this was during the winter months of 1941/42) involved obtaining documents for people I did not know personally, but only from a photograph attached to the documents. At the time, my most important source of free documents was my friend Zbigniew Karnibad, a medical student my own age, who worked in an illegal cell involved in manufacturing forged documents for a section of the Home Army.[3] At the time many members of the various underground organizations as well as Catholic priests were involved in aiding Jews hidden in and around Warsaw and in forging documents. In mid 1942 I established contact with two people, both respected in prewar Poland, who were active in completely different ideological-political areas. One of them, Zofia Kossak-Szatkowska, a Catholic author well known throughout Europe, had been living in Warsaw illegally since the beginning of the Nazi occupation and was wanted by the Gestapo for her anti-Nazi views, which she held before the war; the other, Wanda Krahelska-Filipowicz, was close to socialist circles during her student years and, as a young student before World War I, was responsible for the famous bomb attack on the Russian governor of Warsaw, General Skallon. For many months the two had been heading a secret rescue operation for refugees from the ghetto, mainly for women and children, in which they provided material goods, documents, and shelter. Their large circle of friends and their social standing helped them greatly in this endeavor. They devoted themselves to the undertaking whole-heartedly and gladly welcomed anyone who was willing to risk participating in their undertaking. I began working with Zofia Kossak immediately, and from that point on I frequently played the role of intermediary between her and various persons, Polish Christians as well as Jews, with whom she cooperated. It was my responsibility to deliver documents and money and, if necessary, warnings.

Through the mediation of Ewa Raabe-Wasovicz, a Jew who lived on the "Aryan" side, I met, among others, Leon Feiner, a doctor of law and a member of the board of the Jewish workers' association, the "Bund"; we then worked together for nearly two years. Organizing assistance programs engaged me more and more each month and was soon one of my main occupations. The liquidation of the ghettos that began in central Poland in 1942 represented a development that challenged people of good will to acts of protest and resistance.

At the end of September 1942 the so-called Provisional Konrad Żegota Committee (a cover name) was founded at the initiative of the two women mentioned above, Zofia Kossak and Wanda Krahelska-Filipowicz. The aim of the committee was to organize, continue, and expand the work initiated by individuals willing to take the risk. During the first weeks of its activity, the committee reached about 120 children with its assistance program. About half of them were hiding in Warsaw, a small number were in Kraków, and the remainder were in Kielce, Radom, Lublin, Białystok, and Brest Litovsk. The children were given money, documents, shelter, and even helped to find legal work. In spite of the great effort and the enormous risk the members of the committee took upon themselves, at first their actions were only a drop in the ocean. The necessary preconditions for being able to protect a larger number of persecuted Jews lay in awakening interest in this enterprise in all the democratic political parties of the Polish resistance movement; in establishing contacts with the representatives of the Jewish underground organizations who had just then achieved a working agreement; in quickly obtaining substantial funds from abroad for this program, in view of the general suffering in occupied Poland, through the mediation of the Polish government in exile in London, headed by General Sikorski; and, finally, in establishing an accord with the large Jewish support organizations of the West. These matters obviously depended on making information available to the population in the country through the underground press. Of even greater importance was the need to inform the populations of the Allied nations about the fate of the Jews in Poland. We immediately started to translate this plan into action.

I first met Adolf Berman, a doctor of psychology and the former head of CENTOS, a charitable organization for the protection of children in the Warsaw ghetto, in October of 1942. He had succeeded in escaping from the ghetto at the beginning of September 1942 (after the completion of the brutal "program" executed by SS-*Hauptsturmführer* Hoefle) together with his wife Barbara, who was a social worker. He then established contact with the Polish resistance movement through the mediation of Maria and Stanisław Ossowski, both prominent scientists and professors at the University of Warsaw, and of Wanda Krahelska-Filipowicz. Our meeting took place in an apartment that was used as a safe house and was located at 4 Radna Street on a quiet alley on the Vistula River. Berman was representing various Zionist organizations; I was the delegate of a Catholic group associated with Zofia Kossak which operated under the name Front for Reborn Poland. In addition, Leon Feiner was present as the representative of the "Bund," as was Julian Grobelny, an old socialist functionary. The latter had been sent by the Polish Socialist Party; its numerous former members had been helping their erstwhile Jewish party comrades whenever possible since the beginning of the occupation, especially in Warsaw and Kraków. I seem to remember that the representatives of the Liberal-Democratic Party and the Peasant Party also participated in this conference (or perhaps in the following one). In any case, these people, representing such diverse political directions, quickly achieved a total understanding on the necessity of creating a permanent and vigorous organization to take the place of the Provisory Committee so as to be able to supply extensive aid to the Jews. This agreement was supported by the deputy of the homeland government and thus by the representative of the government in exile, university professor Jan Piekalkiewicz, who was present in Warsaw.[4]

In December 1942 the new organization formally constituted itself as the Council for Aid to Jews (*Rada Pomocy Żydom*). Simultaneously, it adopted the cover name *Żegota* in order to avoid the dangerous use of the word "Jews" in letters and conversations.

The administration of the committee was as follows: Julian Grobelny of the Polish Socialist Party served as chairman; the lawyer Tadeusz Rek of the Peasant Party and Dr. Leon Feiner of the "Bund" served as deputy chairmen; Dr. Adolf Berman, the representative of the Zionist organizations, was secretary; and Ferdynand Marek-Arczyński of the Democratic Party held the office of treasurer. In addition, a permanent liaison was created between the committee and the government representative.

This historic month, December 1942, marked the beginning of the cooperation between the Poles and the Jews to save as many as possible from the death sentence imposed on the whole Jewish people by Nazi Germany. The remarkable growth of the Council for Aid to Jews during the following years of the war, the participation of new political groups (for example, of the leftist-socialist wing), and the creation of smooth-running branches of the Council in Kraków and Lvov are events that merit special attention. The successful attempt to obtain and deliver to the West evidence, collected in the *Black Book*, of the atrocious extermination of the Jews in Poland and to arouse world opinion in the fall of 1942 must be mentioned separately. This was done by workers in Warsaw who were close to the officials who had created the Council for Aid. Even before we founded the underground Council for Aid to Jews, there was a special National Bureau in the Information and Propaganda Office of the headquarters of the Home Army that was very active. This bureau was headed by Stanisław Herbst, who after the war was a professor at the University of Warsaw and the chairman of the Polish Historical Society. It collected material on the situation of the national minorities in occupied Poland, and especially on the Jews. During the winter of 1941/42 a specific bureau was created for Jewish affairs in the Home Army. Its management was entrusted to the legal expert and democratic champion Henryk Woliński (at present a lawyer in Kattowitz) who held the position until the end of the war. When it first began its activities, the Jewish Bureau concentrated for the most part on establishing contacts with the ghettos and camps, especially with the Jewish intelligentsia working in institutions such as cultural associations or hospitals, but also with the workers' functionaries organized in the "Bund," to obtain information earmarked for delivery to the West. Reports on the increasing persecution of the Jews were transmitted to London via the Jewish Bureau of the Home Army. These reports were prepared for the Polish central offices in London as well as for the Jewish delegates representing the Jews of Poland in the parliament in exile — the National Assembly in London. In 1942 the Zionist Dr. Ignacy Schwarzbart and the representative of the "Bund," Szmul Zygielbojm, occupied this office.

In view of the accelerating extermination of the Jews in the crowded ghettos in 1942, it was of great importance to alert the world and to exert the pressure of world opinion on Germany. Clandestine radio stations operated by the Home Army and underground members of the Polish government in Poland time and again broadcast reports on the events in Poland to London during 1942. Initially, however, the trip of a special envoy of the Home Army from Warsaw to England played an important role. This envoy was Jan Kozielewski, who operated under the name Jan Karski. Karski (at present a professor at Georgetown University in Washington, D.C.), who was witness to the liquidation of the Warsaw ghetto in the summer of 1942 and to the mass transports to Treblinka, participated in a conference with representatives of the Zionist organizations and the "Bund" in Warsaw prior to his departure; he was extensively briefed on the situation and given oral instructions for designated officials in England.

I met Karski in August or September of 1942 while the mass extermination in the ghettos was still going on. During our conversations I had the opportunity to observe how deeply he was affected by these horrible crimes.

Karski arrived in London safely in November 1942, where he immediately had the *Black Book* published and took energetic steps to explain the gruesome events in Poland to the leading political circles of Great Britain. He not only held discussions with the Polish prime minister in exile, Sikorski, but also talked to Winston Churchill and distinguished Western intellectuals such as H. G. Wells, Arthur Koestler, and others. (He later described his mission in the book *Story of a Secret State*, published in the United States in 1944.)

Those of us in Warsaw waited impatiently for the results of Karski's trip. The radio soon provided us with this information, for even though the possession of a radio was punishable by death in Poland, broadcasts were not only listened to in the "Aryan" sector and in the ghetto, the contents of the intercepted messages were also published in numerous underground communiqués. On 27 November 1942, soon after Karski's arrival in England, the Polish National Council in London protested against the mass extermination of Poland's Jewish population in a unanimous decision and demanded that the Allies intervene. On 10 December 1942 the acting Polish Department of State in London approached the governments of the countries at war with Hitler with a diplomatic note which stated, among other things, that "it is not sufficient to stigmatize a crime; ways and means have to be found to bring an end to its continuation." Subsequently, the governments of the three great powers — the United States, Great Britain, and the Soviet Union — as well as the Committee of Free France published a unanimous declaration on 17 December 1942 in which they threatened severe punishment for the murderers after the end of the war. In anticipation of the moral reverberations of this event — brought about by the concerted efforts of Polish and Jewish members of the underground movement who had collected the evidence with the help of innumerable nameless informants — we immediately gave this news a great amount of play in our underground press.

The reality of day-to-day life in occupied Poland, however, did not leave us much time to think about the future. The most pressing task was to immediately and continuously uncover all possible ways to help refugees from the ghettos and the transportation trains, orphans, and invalids who needed medical attention. Given the conditions under German occupation, these seemingly simple tasks took up many hours of the time of those willing to help, people who came into contact with the unfathomable misery and the terrible suffering that was the lot of the Jews living in hiding.

According to an estimate made by the Jewish historian Emanuel Ringelblum, there were tens of thousands in hiding in Warsaw alone. At the very least a person living in hiding had to possess a birth certificate, a work permit, and a so-called identity card, a necessary legal document in occupied Poland. The birth certificates could easily be obtained through priests, who, in filling out the documents, used the names of deceased persons whose deaths had not been entered in the parish registers. The identity cards and work permits were obtained as follows: an assumed "Aryan" name was inserted into a blank form that had been stolen by a Polish civil servant for a Jew hiding outside of the ghetto. In case of a random identity check on the street — and bear in mind that these checks were everyday occurrences in Poland at the time — these documents were generally sufficient, especially in the case of women.

More difficult than obtaining forged papers for these people was finding a place for them to live. This was not only because sheltering a Jew was punishable by death, but also because of the exceedingly poor housing conditions of the vast majority of Christian Polish families during the occupation. In addition, nearly every home was threatened or felt pressured by the fact that at least one family member was in a Nazi prison, a camp, in forced labor, or interned. The homes of the Polish intelligentsia as well as those of workers in the city were threatened by searches at any time of the day or night and were under observation as well. Nazi police and SS units looking for fugitive reserve officers, escaped prisoners of war, or juveniles not registered with the employment office frequently found hidden Jews. As a rule, the consequences were tragic: during the Eichmann trial in Jerusalem, Jozef Burzminski, a dentist from Przemyśl, recounted how he had witnessed the extermination of a family of eight by the Nazis because a single Jewish child had been hidden in their house. Professor Kazimierz Kolbuszewski, the most important professor of literature and the former dean of the humanities faculty in Vilnius, was arrested in Lvov for helping his former Jewish students and was killed in the camp at Majdanek in 1943. Numerous peasant families from many towns were shot for hiding Jews. Guided by their humanitarian feelings, the farmers in the area of Galicia, in particular, assisted the Jews they had known before the war.

I myself still clearly remember the day when friends of mine brought a refugee from the camp at Lvov-Janowska, a bookseller from Lvov named Maurycy Gelber, to my home, which was already encumbered by various underground activities. This happened at a time when I intended to leave the apartment since I felt justifiably threatened. I now had to find protection and refuge for Gelber as well. Several of my friends and a number of decent but completely unknown people had to be involved in this affair just to help this one man. Fortunately, he survived and is now living in the United States under a different name.

In spite of our greatest efforts, however, not everyone could be saved. The fate of Emanuel Ringelblum is proof of this. After having been rescued from an extermination camp in 1943 by Christian Poles, he was killed in 1944 together with about thirty other Jews and the Christian family that had given him refuge.

During the second half of 1942, it became apparent that those Jews who had survived and were now living in overcrowded conditions would resist continued Nazi killings. Aided by people with many different outlooks on life — from the center and the left wings of the Zionist movement as well as from the "Bund" — the underground fighting units that had already existed in the Warsaw ghetto in the summer of 1942 were restructured. On 2 December 1942 this coalition officially adopted the name Jewish Combat Organization, with which it made its mark on the history of the European resistance movement. The motivation of the young people who founded the Combat Organization — they were between twenty and thirty years old — was idealistic: "We do not want to save our lives. We know that none of us will get out of here alive, but we want to save our human dignity," Arie Wilner, the representative of the Jewish Combat Organization, explained to one of my friends, Henryk Woliński, the head of the Jewish department of the Home Army, in the fall of 1942. I remember Wilner as one of the most inspiring characters of the Youth Combat movement in the Warsaw ghetto. Sent to the "Aryan" sector to obtain weapons for the fight in the ghetto from the Polish underground movement, he made his way to the Home Army organization with the help of Aleksander Kaminski (after the war a professor at the University of Łódź), a Boy Scout official whom he had known before the war. His enthusiasm, courage, and selflessness gained the respect of all he came in contact with. He fulfilled his mission by obtaining a number of revolvers, several hundred grenades, explosives, and instructions for manufacturing bombs. On 6 March 1943 he was arrested by the Gestapo and, with great pride, admitted to being a member of a Jewish underground organization. In spite of inhuman torture, he did not betray a single address, name, or person. With the help of Christian Polish friends he succeeded in escaping from prison shortly before the outbreak of the

Warsaw ghetto uprising, but he categorically refused to accept the refuge he was offered in the "Aryan" sector. He returned to the ghetto to participate in the fighting and died, a hero, at the side of Anielewicz.

Another Shomer fighter, Jozef Kapłan, who was arrested in the ghetto by the Gestapo in the summer of 1942 on suspicion of membership in an underground organization, wrote before his death in a letter smuggled out of prison: "If we have to die, we will die with dignity."

One of the first proclamations of the Jewish Combat Organization in December 1942 read: "Remember that we, the Jewish civilian population, are at the front of the battle for freedom and humanity!" Toward the end of 1942 the representative body of the Polish government that was active in occupied Poland created a special department, which was to take over the liaison with the Jewish political fighters as well as the humanitarian aid section of the Jewish affairs bureau of the Home Army. The AK — the Home Army — was to continue to deal with the problems of the combat organizations. The head of the new department, "Jan," proposed that I be his deputy, as I had already been in contact with the Zionists and the "Bund" for several months. I accepted this position because I knew how essential it was. I was, however, fearful that I would not be completely equal to it, for at the same time I was to remain on the Council for Aid to Jews. Thus, as of the beginning of 1943, I combined two functions: I was a member of the council that coordinated all the social organizations, and I was the deputy of the representative of the Polish government for Jewish questions. But this did not alter my relations with people: I continued to meet with the representatives of the Polish underground movement and of the secret organizations cooperating with them. From this point to the beginning of the Warsaw uprising in 1944, all of the radio communications and reports of the Jewish underground movement to England, the United States, Palestine, to officials of the World Jewish Congress, to the Zionist World Congress, and to the "Bund" in the free world passed through the underground cell in which I worked, as did the funds that were sent to the Jews in Poland by these organizations.

"The Germans have threatened to execute anyone who helps one of the small numbers of Jews who have managed to escape from their henchmen. Every decent human will treat these threats with contempt, for helping someone in distress, saving a fellow human being menaced by death, is a duty far beyond fear of the death penalty. It is the duty of every Christian Pole to help the victims of German brutality." These are the proud and stirring words with which an illegal newspaper of the Polish Socialist Party introduced itself to the public in the fall of 1942, when the Council for Aid to Jews was in the final stages of organization. This statement was made in direct response to the enactment of a new series of Nazi terror measures intended to put a halt to support given to the Jews.[5] The basic goal of the newly founded Council for Aid to Jews was to create the necessary organizational and financial basis to effectively prevent the complete annihilation of the Jewish people. In this context it should be noted that the members of the Jewish underground movement played an important role in organizing the council and its work. Along with Leon Feiner (of the "Bund"), the deputy chairman of the council, Dr. Adolf Berman, the acting secretary of the council's board, was very active as the representative of the Zionist organizations (in the so-called Jewish National Committee)[6] that were willing to participate. From the time of its conception to the end of the war, Luisa Hausman, before 1939 a lawyer in Stry (formerly East Galicia) then secretly living in Warsaw as "Zofia Rudnicka," was

DER CHEF
des Distrikts Warschau.

Warschau, den 24. 11. 1939.
Palais Brühl.

ANORDNUNG

Betrifft:

Kennzeichnung der Juden

IM DISTRIKT WARSCHAU.

Ich ordne an, dass alle Juden im Alter von über 12 Jahren im Distrikt Warschau mit Wirkung vom 1. 12. 1939 ausserhalb ihrer eigenen Wohnung ein sichtbares Kennzeichen zu tragen haben. Dieser Anordnung unterliegen auch nur vorübergehend im Distriktsbereich anwesende Juden für die Dauer ihres Aufenthaltes.

Als Jude im Sinne dieser Anordnung gilt:

1. wer der mosaischen Glaubensgemeinschaft angehört, oder angehört hat,
2. jeder, dessen Vater oder Muter der mosaischen Glaubensgemeinschaft angehört, oder angehört hat.

Als Kennzeichen ist am rechten Oberarm der Kleidung und der Ueberkleidung eine Armbinde zu tragen, die auf weissem Grunde an der Aussenseite einen blauen Zionstern zeigt. Der weisse Grund muss so gross sein, dass dessen gegenüberliegende Spitzen mindestens 8 cm. entfernt sind. Der Balken muss 1 cm. breit sein.

Juden, die dieser Verpflichtung nicht nachkommen, haben strenge Bestrafung zu gewärtigen.

Für die Ausführung dieser Anordnung, insbesondere die Versorgung der Juden mit Kennzeichen, sind die Aeltestenräte verantwortlich.

Die Durchführung obliegt im Bereich der Stadt Warschau dem Stadtpräsidenten, in den Landkreisen den Kreishauptleuten.

Der Chef des Distrikts Warschau

Dr. FISCHER

Gouverneur.

1. The first directive enacted against the Jews by the German occupying forces in Warsaw, 24 November 1939. (See page 109 for a complete translation of the document.)

2. "Abuses—wild, bestial 'amusements'—are daily events."

3. In places the wall of the ghetto cut across the streets of metropolitan Warsaw. The ghetto was sealed off in November 1940.

4. In the Warsaw ghetto as many as 450,000 people were crammed into a tiny space of approximately 1.5 square miles.

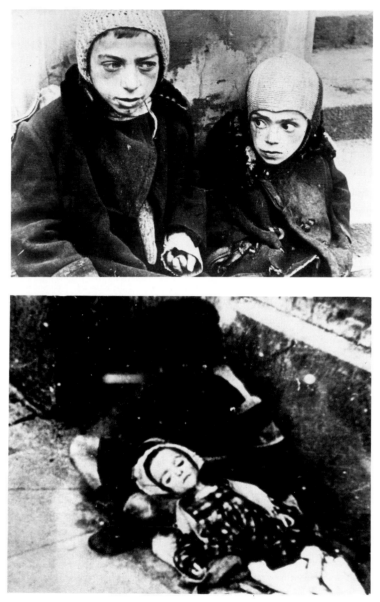

5. Starving and dying children on the streets of the ghetto.

Bekanntmachung

Betr.: Todesstrafe für unbefugtes Verlassen der jüdischen Wohnbezirke.

•

In der letzten Zeit ist durch Juden, die die ihnen zugewiesenen Wohnbezirke verlassen haben, in zahlreichen Fällen nachweislich das Fleckfieber verbreitet worden. Um die hierdurch der Bevölkerung drohende Gefahr abzuwenden, hat der Herr Generalgouverneur verordnet, dass in Zukunft ein Jude, der den ihm zugewiesenen Wohnbezirk unbefugt verlässt, mit dem Tode bestraft wird.

Die gleiche Strafe trifft diejenigen, die diesen Juden wissentlich Unterschlupf gewähren oder in anderer Weise (z. B. durch Gewährung von Nachtlagern, Verpflegung, Mitnahme auf Fahrzeugen aller Art usw.) den Juden behilflich sind.

Die Aburteilung erfolgt durch das Sondergericht Warschau.

Ich weise die gesamte Bevölkerung des Distrikts Warschau auf diese neue gesetzliche Regelung ausdrücklich hin, da nunmehr mit unerbittlicher Strenge vorgegangen wird.

Warschau, am 10. November 1941.

gez. **Dr. FISCHER**
Gouverneur

6. A notice—one among many—of the terror of the German occupation. (See page 110 for a complete translation of the document.)

DER KOMMISSAR
für den jüdischen Wohnbezirk
in Warschau

BEKANNTMACHUNG

Wegen unbefugten Verlassens des jüdischen
Wohnbezirks in Warschau sind die Juden

**Rywka Kligerman
Sala Pasztejn
Josek Pajkus
Luba Gac
Motek Fiszbaum
Fajga Margules
Dwojra Rozenberg
Chana Zajdenwach**

durch Urteil des Sondergerichts Warschau vom 12. November 1941
zum Tode verurteilt worden.

Das Urteil ist am 17. November 1941 vollstreckt worden.

ges. *Auerswald*

KOMISARZ
dla dzielnicy żydowskiej
w Warszawie

Bek Nr. 441

Warszawa, dnia 17 listopada 1941 r.

OBWIESZCZENIE

Za nieuprawnione opuszczenie dzielnicy żydowskiej w Warszawie zostali żydzi

**Rywka Kligerman
Sala Pasztejn
Josek Pajkus
Luba Gac
Motek Fiszbaum
Fajga Margules
Dwojra Rozenberg
Chana Zajdenwach**

em Sądu Specjalnego w Warszawie z dnia 12 listopada 1941 r. skazani na śmierć.
Wyrok został wykonany dnia 17 listopada 1941 r.

( ) *Auerswald*

7. Court-ordered executions were also announced for the purpose of intimidation. (See page 111 for a partial translation of the document.)

ANORDNUNG

Betrifft:

Kennzeichnung der Juden

IM DISTRIKT WARSCHAU.

Ich ordne an, dass alle Juden im Alter von über 12 Jahren im Distrikt Warschau mit Wirkung vom 1. 12. 1939 ausserhalb ihrer eigenen Wohnung ein sichtbares Kennzeichen zu tragen haben. Dieser Anordnung unterliegen auch nur vorübergehend im Distriktsbereich anwesende Juden für die Dauer ihres Aufenthaltes.

Als Jude im Sinne dieser Anordnung gilt:

1. wer der mosaischen Glaubensgemeinschaft angehört, oder angehört hat,
2. jeder, dessen Vater oder Mutter der mosaischen Glaubensgemeinschaft angehört, oder angehört hat.

Als Kennzeichen ist am rechten Oberarm der Kleidung und der Ueberkleidung eine Armbinde zu tragen, die auf weissem Grunde an der Aussenseite einen blauen Zionstern zeigt. Der weisse Grund muss so gross sein, dass dessen gegenüberliegende Spitzen mindestens 8 cm. entfernt sind. Der Balken muss 1 cm. breit sein.

Juden, die dieser Verpflichtung nicht nachkommen, haben strenge Bestrafung zu gewärtigen.

Für die Ausführung dieser Anordnung, insbesondere die Versorgung der Juden mit Kennzeichen, sind die Aeltestenräte verantwortlich.

Die Durchführung obliegt im Bereich der Stadt Warschau dem Stadtpräsidenten, in den Landkreisen den Kreishauptleuten.

Der Chef des Distrikts Warschau

Dr. FISCHER

Gouverneur.

1. The first directive enacted against the Jews by the German occupying forces in Warsaw, 24 November 1939. (See page 109 for a complete translation of the document.)

2. "Abuses—wild, bestial 'amusements'—are daily events."

3. In places the wall of the ghetto cut across the streets of metropolitan Warsaw. The ghetto was sealed off in November 1940.

4. In the Warsaw ghetto as many as 450,000 people were crammed into a tiny space of approximately 1.5 square miles.

5. Starving and dying children on the streets of the ghetto.

Bekanntmachung

Betr.: Todesstrafe für unbefugtes Verlassen der jüdischen Wohnbezirke.

•

In der letzten Zeit ist durch Juden, die die ihnen zugewiesenen Wohnbezirke verlassen haben, in zahlreichen Fällen nachweislich das Fleckfieber verbreitet worden. Um die hierdurch der Bevölkerung drohende Gefahr abzuwenden, hat der Herr Generalgouverneur verordnet, dass in Zukunft ein Jude, der den ihm zugewiesenen Wohnbezirk unbefugt verlässt, mit dem Tode bestraft wird.

Die gleiche Strafe trifft diejenigen, die diesen Juden wissentlich Unterschlupf gewähren oder in anderer Weise (z. B. durch Gewährung von Nachtlagern, Verpflegung, Mitnahme auf Fahrzeugen aller Art usw.) den Juden behilflich sind.

Die Aburteilung erfolgt durch das Sondergericht Warschau.

Ich weise die gesamte Bevölkerung des Distrikts Warschau auf diese neue gesetzliche Regelung ausdrücklich hin, da nunmehr mit unerbittlicher Strenge vorgegangen wird.

Warschau, am 10. November 1941.

gez. Dr. FISCHER
Gouverneur

6. A notice—one among many—of the terror of the German occupation. (See page 110 for a complete translation of the document.)

BEKANNTMACHUNG

Wegen unbefugten Verlassens des jüdischen Wohnbezirks in Warschau sind die Juden

**Rywka Kligerman
Sala Pasztejn
Josek Pajkus
Luba Gac
Motek Fiszbaum
Fajga Margules
Dwojra Rozenberg
Chana Zajdenwach**

durch Urteil des Sondergerichts Warschau vom 12. November 1941 **zum Tode verurteilt worden.**

Das Urteil ist am 17. November 1941 vollstreckt worden.

gez. *Auerswald*

KOMISARZ
dla dzielnicy żydowskiej
w Warszawie

Warszawa, dnia 17 listopada 1941 r

Bek Nr. 44

OBWIESZCZENIE

Za nieuprawnione opuszczenie dzielnicy żydowskiej w Warszawie zostali żydzi

**Rywka Kligerman
Sala Pasztejn
Josek Pajkus
Luba Gac
Motek Fiszbaum
Fajga Margules
Dwojra Rozenberg
Chana Zajdenwach**

em Sądu Specjalnego w Warszawie z dnia 12 listopada 1941 r. skazani na śmierć.
Wyrok został wykonany dnia 17 listopada 1941 r.

( ) *Auerswald*

7. Court-ordered executions were also announced for the purpose of intimidation. (See page 111 for a partial translation of the document.)

the head of the underground office of the Council. She was entrusted with many of the conspiratorial matters relating to the assistance program. The female liaison officers included Polish Christians as well as Jews; they were continually moving money and forged documents from one place to another under the scrutiny of the most brutal police controls. (One of the most courageous of these women was Ewa Wasovicz, whom I mentioned earlier.) The cooperation between people of different backgrounds and convictions (Poles and Jews, socialists and Catholics) was very close within the Council for Aid to Jews and the organization functioned harmoniously. Political views were not the determining factor in these circumstances; a person's ethical stance was what counted, as all of us participating in this work during the occupation had ample opportunity to find out.

Adolf Berman, Jitzchak Cukierman, and D. Kaftor wrote the following in a report sent to Dr. Schwarzbart in London by secret courier, a report which I, among others, also read at the time:

The Jewish National Committee is participating in the work of the Council for Aid to Jews in the Polish Government Delegacy. Its secretary is a representative of the Jewish National Committee. In addition, the Jewish National Committee is in close contact with the (Jewish) Office for National Minorities in the Government Delegacy and with the Office for Jewish Affairs in the command of the Armed Forces in the Homeland [Home Army]. The Jewish National Committee is cooperating with the representatives of the fighting Polish underground movement in a close and sincere relationship.

In its activities, the Council for Aid to Jews attempted to help the Jews living illegally in the "Aryan" sector as well as those Jews in the ghettos and work camps still

in existence in 1943. This program developed gradually
but systematically, and after the Council had been in
existence for about one year, it was able to provide
continuous care for at least 4,000 people in Warsaw
alone. This does not include the aid provided in Kraków,
Lvov, and in the other small cities. Every organization
represented in the Council was responsible for the support of a certain number of people, and every month
the Council distributed financial support to the Jews
living outside the ghetto through Council cells that had
been established within the various organizations of the
resistance movement. These cells also soon formed
among various professional groups, including teachers,
physicians, lawyers, and journalists, who helped a given
number of their Jewish colleagues and their families who
were living in hiding. In Warsaw, the Council organized
a so-called Legalization Bureau, where forged documents were manufactured for free distribution to those
it attempted to help. This led to a great advance in the
quantity as well as the quality of the forged documents
in comparison to the period prior to the creation of the
Council, when documents had to be obtained privately.
The "legalization activity" of the Council expanded to
such a degree that a few months saw the creation of
several thousand different documents and certificates. A
housing office was also created, one of the main tasks
of which was to find living quarters for those in hiding,
a practically endless activity, since the need was so much
greater than the available space. This office was headed
by the architectural engineer Emilia Hizowa, who had
been a social activist before the war. When the need
arose we would all help, the members of the Council as
well as people who had only a superficial association
with it. From my own experience, I remember the frequent necessity of moving people in hiding from one
location to another because their houses were being

watched by the Germans or by people suspected of collaborating with them.

The duties of the Council included attending to elderly people, sick refugees from the prisons and camps, pregnant women, and children; also requiring attention were cases of sudden illness, for example broken arms or legs, or infectious diseases. Providing medical help to a Jew was also punishable by death. Within the framework of the Council, we organized an office for medical aid headed by Dr. Ludwig Rostkowski, an ophthalmologist (after the war he became a university lecturer in medicine in Warsaw). He created a secret medical support network with a group of his colleagues, mainly internists, pediatricians, and surgeons. The physicians working in this program visited and treated patients living in hiding free of charge and, if necessary, found a space for them in a hospital.

Taking care of orphans and children who had been separated from their parents was especially difficult. The Council, as well as the Jewish underground organizations, gave special attention to this problem. The children were placed individually with Polish families or in groups in various homes, hospitals, orphanages, or in the municipal and charity institutions that still existed. Catholic convents played a great role in helping with these problems, above all the Ursulines, the Franciscans, the Carmelites, and the Servites. The employees of the autonomous Polish social institutions — which had in many cases been close to the socialist movement before the war — also supplied active support. Irena Sendlerowa (after the war a school principal in Warsaw), an experienced staff member of the legal municipal welfare office, was the head of the children's protection office within the Council.

During the first months of its activity the Council had very limited means at its disposal for its support program. The regular subsidy from the Polish government in exile in London, transferred to the Council by the underground representation it had designated, started at 250,000 zlotys a month at the beginning of 1943, was later increased to a half a million zlotys, and finally reached one million zlotys in 1944. But the buying power of the zloty was minimal during the occupation. At the time, the average income of a civil servant was 300 to 500 zlotys a month, which amounted to starvation wages. Considering that, in addition to being forced to pay for their quarters as subletters, Jews living in hiding frequently did not possess food cards, the support of 300 and later 500 zlotys a month granted by the Council was just enough for the most meager existence. Caring for children and the sick was even more expensive. In addition, the Council developed contacts with the camps in Poniatow, Trawniki, Plaszow, Lvov-Janowska, Pustkow near Debica, and Skarżysko-Kamienna, and searched out ways (frequently through the mediation of legally existing welfare organizations) of sending additional food and, in individual cases, funds to the inhabitants of the camps. At times the possibility of buying an individual out of the camp also arose, as the corruption of the Nazi appartus was slowly becoming endemic. This possibility, however, was rare and was usually resorted to to save people who were known in Jewish cultural or scientific circles. These cases always absorbed sums of several tens of thousands of zlotys. A so-called Provincial Office, which played an important organizational role in these instances, was headed by a well-known socialist from the administrative district of Lublin, Stefan Sendlak.

"We are only a handful of old fighters who have stayed alive and who have set ourselves the goal of providing social services to the remaining Jewish population that has survived in spite of the steadily increasing dangers and difficulties," the representatives of the Zionist organizations in Warsaw wrote in November of 1943 in the report for Dr. Schwarzbart in London. "We are determined to carry this task through to its final conclusion regardless of all the difficulties and obstacles."

These "difficulties and obstacles" could not have been overcome without extensive financial means, even with the greatest personal willingness to sacrifice on the part of the Polish Christians and Jews participating in the aid program. The contributions the Polish people, impoverished as they were by the occupation, could make were much too small. The funds transferred by the Polish government in London were not sufficient. Thus the financial help coming from the Jewish world organizations was of the greatest importance; it could even be said that it brought about a turning point in 1943. The contributions from these organizations were transferred to occupied Poland through the Polish government in London. Thousands of Jewish families in Poland received individual American Joint Distribution Committee help in the form of food and clothing packages as well as financial support from the neutral countries as of the first months of the occupation, even before the ghettos were closed and the mass extermination programs began. After the whole of Jewish society was driven into illegality, the underground movement was responsible for receiving and distributing the Jewish aid from the countries of the free world.

I no longer have the necessary documentation that would show the amounts the American Joint Distribution Committee, the World Jewish Congress, and other Zionist organizations as well as the "Bund" made available in the United States and Great Britain to help Polish Jews. Partially preserved transcripts of reports and documents of those years indicate, for example, that the Zionist organizations received at least $96,000 from abroad between June of 1943 and the end of that year. I am also aware of an amount of approximately $5,000 for an earlier period (the first half of 1943).

During the second half of 1942 the "Bund" received about $10,000 and at least $48,000 in 1943. It has to be said that these funds were used only for defensive purposes (the purchase of weapons) and humanitarian aid, without any kind of deductions for administrative costs, etc.

The Jewish organizations transferred a portion of all financial aid from abroad to the Council for Aid to Jews for distribution among its protégés; they disposed of the remainder themselves through their own channels.

Adolf Berman, Jitzchak Cukierman, and D. Kaftor wrote to Dr. Schwarzbart in London on behalf of all the underground Zionist organizations in Poland:

We wish to express our deeply felt thanks for these funds in the name of all of our organizations. They will enable us to expand the range of our assistance and rescue operations. Unfortunately, this help came too late for many of our brothers. It is, however, our hope that we will be able to rescue many valuable lives and ease the heavy lot of many thousands with the aid of these funds.

The influx of aid from the Jewish organizations abroad had a visible effect on the quality of the help provided. Above all, we were able to assist a large number of people (the personal resources of many of the Jews living in hiding, who had not needed help at the beginning of the occupation, had been exhausted by now). In addition, we were able to provide better care for the children in hiding. Finally — and this was of the greatest importance — the year 1943 saw a considerable increase in the area covered by the activities of the Council and, simultaneously, an expansion of the direct contacts between the Jewish organizations and those people in various parts of occupied Poland who were awaiting help from the Council.

A branch of the Council for Aid to Jews was established in Kraków in March of 1943. To a great extent, the Kraków Council was managed by socialists and members of the Peasant Party. It was headed by Stanisław Dobrowolski, a lawyer in the Polish Socialist Party, who after the war joined the diplomatic service of the People's Republic of Poland, where he served as, among other things, ambassador to Denmark and Greece. Dr. Tadeusz Seweryn (who after the war became professor of ethnography at Jagiellonian University and the director of the Ethnographic Museum in Kraków) was also important to the Council's work. The representative of the Jewish community on the Kraków Council, Maria Hochberg-Marianska, was very active and noted for her courage (after the war she was an independent journalist and an assistant at Yad Vashem's branch office in Tel Aviv; she now goes by the name of Miriam Peleg).

Even before the Council for Aid was founded in Kraków, a group of socialists (including Jozef Cyrankiewicz, Zygmunt Klopotowski, and Adam Rysiewicz) organized systematic aid for Jewish socialists there. With the consent of Archbishop Adam Sapieha, the Catholic clergy and several monasteries participated in the aid program as well. After the Council had been established in Kraków, it was able to expand the extent of its activities. With support from Warsaw and with donations from Jewish organizations abroad, the Council succeeded in establishing contacts with several work camps and was thus able to provide money and food. This aid went to, among others, those being held in the camp at Plaszow and to the prisoners working at German plants in the city. With the help of the Council, several refugees from the camps were moved to Kraków where they could be cared for. The renowned author Michał Borwicz, who succeeded in escaping from the Lvov-Janowska camp, should be mentioned here (at present he is active in the scientific and literary fields in Paris). Various escape routes were used: the socialist fighters Adam Rysiewicz and Marian Bomba, who were in contact with the Kraków Council, took about fifty people from Poland across the border into Hungary in 1943, where the living conditions were still much better than in occupied Poland. Because of the good relations between the Council and the farmers of the administrative district of Kraków, it was possible to shelter more people in the countryside there than in other administrative districts.

In 1943 a group of Lvov's Polish intelligentsia which had its roots in democratic and socialist circles and in the Home Army, and which had been involved in helping the Jews in Lvov since 1941, created a branch of the Warsaw main office of the Council. Władysława Chomsowa, who was wholeheartedly dedicated to the cause of saving refugees, deserves great credit for her participation. Kurt Grossmann dedicated a chapter with the expressive title "The Angel of Lvov" in his beautiful book *The Unsung Heroes* to her self-sacrificing deeds. Chomsowa was among the group of Poles who were honored in Israel with the designation "Chassidey Umoth Haolam" ("The Just among the Peoples of the World"). In 1963 she planted one of the young trees on Jerusalem's Mount of Remembrance. But the financial help given to the Jews of Poland by foreign Jewish organizations during the occupation is not the only matter worth recalling. The incredible moral and ideological importance that maintaining contacts with the free world had for those who were leading the underground fight against Nazi barbarism must not be forgotten either.

According to official Nazi statistics, after the great extermination campaign in the Warsaw ghetto during the summer of 1942, there were still approximately 35,000 Jews living outside of the ghetto walls. These people supplied forced labor in the factories and workshops of such companies as W. C. Toebbens, Schultz, Bernhard Hallmann, and others. Men, women, and children were mercilessly exploited by these companies in conditions of literal slavery. About the same number of people, who had been declared unproductive by the Germans, lived in the ghetto illegally. Only a few of the several hundred people who had originally been involved with the underground organizations in the ghetto during the summer of 1942 were still in Warsaw. The "resettlement" to the gas chambers of Treblinka had paralyzed the nascent underground in the ghetto. Since those who survived were mainly young, able-bodied people, a new situation arose in the fall of 1942 which led to the creation of a homogeneous Jewish combat organization. This organization defined the main goals of its activities in its statutes of December 1942:

1. Resistance, including the use of force, to new "resettlement programs" by the Germans (with the slogan "We will not let you have a single Jew").
2. Carrying out terrorist actions against traitors collaborating with the Germans to the detriment of the Jewish population.

A second organization operating in the ghetto called the Jewish Army Alliance (created by the Zionist-Revisionists, prewar members of the Betar organization), set identical goals for itself.

One of the first declarations of the Jewish Combat Organization to be circulated in the ghetto, which I was initially made aware of by Adolf Berman in December of 1942, was a categorical warning not to believe any statements or promises made by the Nazis:

The uncertainty of tomorrow poisons every moment of the bitter life of the prisoners in the Jewish district of Warsaw. Every day brings new news, rumors, gossip, and new deadlines concerning the fate of the ghetto. They "give" us two, three, four months to live. Frayed nerves are torn between hope and desperation.

Has our terrible experience taught us nothing? Will we still let ourselves be deluded by a kind word from one or another Nazi killer, from some Jewish Gestapo man, from hirelings or traitors, or by a rumor spread by the credulous? There can be no doubt that Nazism has set itself the goal of exterminating all Jews. Its tactics are based on deceit and hypocrisy. It cuts the throat of one victim and toys with the fate of the next before leading him to slaughter. Let us face the truth openly and courageously! . . .

Jews! Citizens of the Warsaw ghetto, be alert! Do not believe a single word, a single pretext of the SS bandits! Mortal danger awaits!

Let us stop giving in to illusions! . . .

The Germans have once again found collaborators and servants among the Jewish population. Do not believe the Jewish traitors, the foremen, the bosses! They are your enemies! Do not let them deceive you!

Do not convince yourselves and do not let anyone else convince you that the better artisans, the older workers who have a number are safe, and that those who are weaker or defenseless must therefore be sacrificed!

Everyone is in danger!

Do not even consider actively or passively helping to betray friends, neighbors, or colleagues into the hands of the henchmen. We will not be a heap of dirt, worms, in the face of destruction!

Help each other!

We must remove from our midst the worthless traitors who help the enemy!

Do not let yourselves be slaughtered!

Prepare to defend your own lives! Bear in mind that we, too — the Jewish civilian population — are at the forefront of the battle for freedom and humanity!

In places the enemy is already weak. Let us defend our honor with courage and dignity! Let liberty live!

The Jewish Military Association, the second largest organization in the Warsaw ghetto, and which had been created by right-leaning political groups, adopted an identical position. In an appeal in January 1943 it called for a "ruthless fight against the occupation to the last drop of blood."

These declarations fittingly expressed the growing mood among the Warsaw Jews, and the declarations were followed by actions. At the end of 1942 and the beginning of 1943 the two combat organizations executed traitors and Gestapo collaborators in the ghetto; more than sixty especially pernicious informers and provocateurs were liquidated.

To us, Christian Poles in the underground movement who were in constant contact with representatives of the Jewish resistance movement in the "Aryan" sector, the deeply idealistic nature of the actions and goals of the Jewish organizations appeared eminently characteristic. During the winter of 1942/43 we discussed with the representatives of the underground movement a proposal aimed at partially saving the ghetto in a meeting of the Council for Aid to Jews. We offered to find hiding places with Christian Poles for those "important" people — from a cultural, intellectual, and social point of view — still living and for the children in the "Aryan" sector. The Jewish combat organizations and the political branches of the underground movement associated with them considered this proposal and decided against the plan. They felt that all adult inhabitants of the ghetto should participate in the struggle.

They decided that only children and those individuals who would be of no use while the ghetto was being mobilized because of age or health should go. This attitude on the part of our friends on the other side of the wall earned our respect, even if it was debatable. It was specifically in this context that, on several occasions during the war as well as afterwards, I found it necessary to point out to people who were not familiar with the problem of the Warsaw ghetto uprising that the battle, after months of systematic preparations, was not an act of desperation chosen for lack of other options. The opposite was in fact true: the chief organizers and leaders of the uprising were people who could easily have saved their own lives, who had secure contacts with the Polish underground movement, and a good chance of surviving the war among the Christian Polish population. The leaders of the Jewish resistance movement made the decision to fight mainly for idealistic reasons and prepared those taking part in it accordingly.

At the beginning of April 1943 the Hechaluz and Hashomer organizations, through our services, sent a radiogram with the following message to Tel Aviv (in care of Tabenkin and Yaari, the leaders of the Chaluz and Shomer movements in Palestine): "Those of our supporters who still survive are fighting for the honor of the remaining Jewry in Poland." Anielewicz himself, the twenty-four-year old commander of the Jewish Combat Organization, appealed to the Jews of Warsaw:

Large numbers of us, perhaps thousands, should be prepared. We will unify into an army. It makes no difference who you

are and how you feel — if you have a proud spirit and a heart
that has not been contaminated by the filthy poison of the street,
join us! Stand shoulder to shoulder with us in the battle for the
life of these hopeless, condemned masses.

At the beginning of January 1943 the news of Himmler's arrival spread through Warsaw. Based on the sad
experiences of the previous year, we knew that this visit
could presage nothing good. And that was indeed the
case: in mid January, on a cold Sunday, SS and police
formations organized immense raids in the Aryan sector
on a scale thus far unknown. People were dragged from
their homes and out of streetcars, they were arrested in
front of churches. Thousands of Christian Poles fell victim to this operation as well, some of whom were
shipped directly to the Majdanek concentration camp
near Lublin without any kind of hearing or investigation;
others were taken to Germany as forced laborers.

As early as 18 January 1943, almost simultaneously
with these terrorist raids, the Nazis began a new "resettlement" in the ghetto. This time only a few people
reported to the transportation point. In some places in
the ghetto bitter fighting broke out; in some cases members of the Jewish Combat Organization voluntarily
joined the columns of people being led to the transportation point to offer armed resistance at the appropriate
moment. The number of weapons available at the time
to the young people in the Jewish Combat Organization
was not large. But the pistols that Arie Wilner had received from the Home Army were put to use. The resistance offered by the fighters came as a complete
surprise to the myrmidons of the Gestapo and the police.

At the end of January 1943 one of the Polish underground newspapers, *Dzien* ("The Day"), reported the

following in an article entitled "How the Warsaw Ghetto Is Defending Itself":

The street was in the hands of the Jewish fighters for fifteen to twenty minutes. Only large reinforcements of the police enabled the Germans to gain control of the situation. The armed resistance made an extraordinarily strong impression on the whole ghetto; it was received with great enthusiasm by the whole Jewish community. The old Jews blessed the fighters. The bodies of the dead were kissed on the street.

The journal of the Home Army, the *Biuletyn Informacyjny* (no. 4, 28 January 1943), gave its impression of the recent events in the ghetto:

The German police, encountering resistance, responded with gunfire and grenades, killing hundreds of people, but they were afraid to go into the defended buildings. The organized points of resistance defended themselves on Monday and Tuesday. They only retreated when faced by two SS squadrons that had been brought into the ghetto on Wednesday in full combat readiness with machine guns, mortars, and ambulances. A blood bath ensued among the population, which, incited by the events of the previous days, offered active resistance with the aid of the most primitive of means such as iron rods, bars, and stones. This resistance was bloodily suppressed by the SS. The German losses were ten dead police and SS troops and an equal number of Jewish police. The German action was terminated on Thursday. The ghetto is expecting its resumption at any moment.

Of the fifty units of the Jewish Combat Organization that existed in January of 1943, only five remained after four days of fighting. The others were wiped out during the action or captured and deported. For the first time, though, the Nazis suffered losses as well. And for the

first time the Germans were forced to stop their operation: surprised by the resistance, they contented themselves with the deportation of 6,500 people, and then
retreated from the ghetto.

The effect of the ghetto uprising of January 1943,
reported by the underground press with great admiration, was considerable on two counts: first, it served to
boost morale because it was an indicator of the true
mood of the inhabitants of the Jewish quarter and because it served as an example to those who had not thus
far joined the combat organization; it also had a material
effect because as a result the Polish Home Army decided
to give the ghetto a number of pistols, hand grenades,
and a large quantity of explosives in the belief that the
weapons, so invaluable during the occupation, would
be put to good use.

Before the outbreak of the fighting of January 1943
Adolf Berman had delivered a radiogram to the Jewish
office of the representatives of the Polish government.
The message was jointly addressed to the American Jewish Congress, the World Jewish Congress, and the American Joint Distribution Committee, and was passed on
to London. In this telegram, the Jewish National Committee, representing all of the Zionist organizations of
Poland, supplied up-to-date information on the Nazi
extermination campaign. It also made a number of demands, the most important of which was for reprisals
against the Germans and for the taking of action to stop
the mass extermination; in addition it asked for the rescue of 10,000 children through an exchange, and for
$500,000 for defense and aid. At the beginning of Feb-
ruary of 1943 we forwarded a telegram from the Central
Committee of the "Bund" for radio broadcast. It was
addressed to Szmul Zygielbojm, the chairman of the
"Bund" in London and was signed by Feiner and Orzech.
This telegram reported on the armed resistance of the

ghetto and demanded: "Alarm the whole world. Work toward an official intervention by the Pope, prevail on the Allies to treat the German prisoners of war as hostages." As the future would show, with the exception of financial support, these demands unfortunately proved to be impossible to fulfill.

No doubt counting too much on the Germans' despondency after their defeat at Leningrad, the Jewish fighters and the authors of these telegrams, and we ourselves, who first read the messages and transmitted them to the free world, still harbored certain hopes at the beginning of 1943, and yielded to the illusion that international intervention could be at least partially successful.

Meanwhile, important new events took place almost daily. The resistance of the Warsaw ghetto intensified continually and visibly after January 1943, and expressed itself in various ways. When Walter Toebbens, the chief Nazi authority in matters of employment and resettlement in the ghetto, tried to persuade a group of men who worked in the so-called *Schuppen* ("shed") to leave Warsaw voluntarily for an unknown destination during February and March of 1943, the response was appropriate: during the night of 18/19 February, the glare of fire spread over the ghetto; Jewish fighters had torched a large warehouse full of furniture worth several million zlotys that had been readied for shipment to Germany. A second act of sabotage was committed on 6 March 1943: enormous SS warehouses on Nalewki Street went up in flames. SS troops and Nazi police died on the streets of the ghetto. The power in the ghetto slipped from the control of the official Nazi administration almost completely, and the authority of the underground organization grew in importance. Not even the Nazi minions could ignore this fact: at one point Toebbens even felt it necessary to publish a declaration in which he discussed the principles of the Jewish Combat Organization! The time when the Warsaw Jews had obeyed German proclamations and directives was past. The ghetto was feverishly working on the construction of hidden bunkers and subterranean fortifications. We were continuously receiving confidential news about German preparations for the final destruction of the ghetto from various sources, although Himmler's secret order of 16 February 1943, sealing the fate of the Jews who had survived so far and of the ghetto itself, was obviously unknown to us.[7]

By the beginning of February the Jewish Combat Organization commanded twenty-two combat squadrons (from a few to several dozen people) in the Warsaw ghetto, including several hundred persons who were prepared to face anything. The organizations united in the ZKN supplied eighteen squadrons, among them fourteen Zionist-socialist and four communist squadrons; four squadrons were composed of members of the "Bund."

"Nine squadrons were concentrated in the center of the ghetto, eight in the area of the Toebbens and Schultz workshops, five in the ghetto of the *Bürstemachershop*. At the time we received a large shipment of weapons from the Polish military authorities." Thus reads a 1943 report prepared by the command of the Jewish Combat Organization on the Warsaw ghetto uprising which was transmitted to Great Britain by the Polish underground and printed in foreign newspapers while the war was still going on. The weapons shipment mentioned is certainly a reference to the supplies delivered to the Jewish Combat Organization from the depot of the Warsaw district of the Home Army during the winter of 1942/43 and the first quarter of 1943. Seventy pistols with magazines and ammunition, 500 grenades, highly volatile explosives including fuses and detonators, materials for making Molotov cocktails, and hand grenades were supplied. A second shipment included a machine gun, a tommy gun, twenty pistols with magazines and ammunition, 100 hand grenades, and diversion materials such as time bombs and delayed action fuses. In addition, the representatives of the ghetto ran an extended purchase program for weapons and ammunition, approaching any and every source. The secret production of grenades and Molotov cocktails by Michał Klepfisz, an engineer and member of the "Bund" in the Warsaw ghetto, was also of considerable importance.[8]

At the beginning of 1943 those of us in Warsaw did not have the slightest idea that we would soon be witnesses to the hitherto most heroic and stunning event in the history of the resistance to the occupying forces in Poland: the armed April revolt of the Warsaw ghetto.

On 13 March shots were once again fired in the streets of the Warsaw ghetto: a Jewish combat group was offering armed resistance to the police and to members of the German Industrial Protection Unit engaged in looting. In retribution, the SS mowed down several dozen people on the street. The command of the Jewish Combat Organization in the ghetto posted flyers during the night of 14/15 March informing the population of a new "action" being planned.

We soon found out that the tragic fate of the Jewish community in Kraków had been sealed on 13 March. There were still about 10,000 people living in the ghetto there who had survived the June and October 1942 "resettlements" to the extermination camps. Now some of them — those who had been declared able-bodied — were killed on the spot or sent to their deaths in Auschwitz; some were taken to the camp in Plaszow near Kraków, where they were forced into slave labor that ultimately proved fatal. Only a few individuals were saved. These survivors had been sheltered by Christian Poles in Kraków and its surroundings with the help of

Christian friends or by establishing contacts with the Council for Aid to Jews in Kraków. Dr. Julian Aleksandrowicz, an outstanding hematologist, was one of those who managed to escape from the Kraków ghetto during those critical days in March. He later participated in the fight against the Germans as a member of the Home Army. He is now an academic known throughout Europe and professor emeritus at the Hospital for Internal Medicine at the Kraków Medical Academy.

The alarming news from Kraków increased the anxiety of those of us in Warsaw. In view of our experiences during the past few years we were well aware of the fact that Berlin's centrally coordinated extermination campaigns were guided by an ulterior criminal purpose and that the Warsaw ghetto, which still had 70,000 inhabitants, would soon be a target. But the members of the two Jewish combat groups, the Jewish Combat Organization and the Jewish Military Association, were not wasting any time: the network of bunkers and fortifications was expanded systematically; considerable numbers of Molotov cocktails and hand grenades were manufactured according to the guidelines supplied by the Polish Home Army.

The spring of 1943 came early. April was mild and generally warm, and there was relatively heavy traffic on the streets of Warsaw. The Easter holidays were imminent, as was Passover. On Palm Sunday, 18 April 1943, rumors spread through Warsaw that a large police action was to take place in the ghetto during the next few hours. The rumors were underscored by, among other things, a considerable concentration of the collaborating Ukrainian-Latvian support units in the city. In the evening, shortly before the curfew for Christian Poles, I went to the vicinity of the ghetto wall and noted an increased number of police patrols, which were also immediately noticed by the vigilant reconnaissance troops of the Jewish Combat Organization in the ghetto. They alarmed the combat groups, who took up their positions during the same night; the majority of the civilian population hid in their cellars.

"No one got any sleep during the night from Sunday to Monday," a participant in the events, an official of the Jewish National Committee, recalls in a report published in June of 1943 in the underground Catholic monthly *Prawda*.

The combat groups posted sentries. The civilian population retreated into shelters, cellars, or upper floors. The apartments were empty. The first reports of the observers came in: the walls of the ghetto were surrounded by German troops. So it *was* an action.

Several hours later, at daybreak on 19 April — the fourteenth day of Nissan, Erew Pesach — 850 SS troops and sixteen officers of the *Waffen*-SS marched into the ghetto protected by tanks and two armored cars. They moved along Nalewki Street — the main artery of the Jewish residential area — in the direction of the center of the ghetto. After they had gone a few hundred meters they had already encountered unexpected resistance: young members of the Jewish Combat Organization threw hand grenades and Molotov cocktails out of the windows of the adjoining houses. One of the tanks was hit and went up in flames; twelve Nazis were killed on the street, and the SS column hurriedly retreated from the ghetto. The Germans resumed the fight again after two hours, this time with greater caution and larger forces. SS brigade commander Jürgen Stroop, the major general of the police, took over the command.

Because the ghetto uprising has been discussed so frequently in the literature, it is difficult to discuss so encompassing a topic as the weeks of fighting between Jews and Germans in Warsaw in so short a space. Without a doubt, this battle is among the most unusual and heroic episodes in the history of Hitler-occupied Europe. I will limit myself here to more personal memories. At the time I was living in Zoliborz, a suburb of Warsaw located to the north of the ghetto. On the morning of 19 April, immediately after I had left my apartment, I was told of the fighting in the ghetto by some people working on the streetcar. Rumors of tanks destroyed by the Jews were already circulating through the city, and the losses inflicted on the Germans by the defenders of the ghetto were being openly discussed with great satisfaction. I immediately went to a building that was the seat of the Jewish office of the delegation of the Polish government in exile and that served as one of the regular locations for our meetings with the members of the Jewish underground movement.[9]

As coincidence would have it, this place was only a few hundred meters away from the three-meter-high wall of the ghetto near Bonifraterska Street. The ghetto reverberated with the piercing chatter of machine guns and occasional loud explosions. SS troops, the police, and the support troops of the collaborators were standing near the wall in tight rows. Time and again tanks and cars with supplies for the Nazis drove by, while German ambulances moved in the opposite direction. While talking to Leon Feiner and Adolf Berman, who came by later, we heard new gunfire and explosions which were coming from a battery of light artillery of the *Wehrmacht* that had taken up its position on a square near the ghetto and was being used against the insurgents with all the efficiency of the German war machine.

Any kind of personal contact with the fighters in the ghetto was out of the question since it had been surrounded by a tight German cordon. After a short discussion, we went into the city with Berman and Feiner to obtain as much information about the situation as possible since it was important to broadcast the information to the West immediately. During the afternoon Berman supplied us with the first communiqué from the Jewish National Committee that was drafted on the Polish side.

In the meantime events took their course. In the evening a unit of about twenty Christian Polish soldiers of the Home Army — under orders of the Warsaw command of the Home Army — attacked the ghetto wall and attempted to break through it. The unit was under the command of Jozef Pszenny, a captain of the engineers.[10] A bitter fight between the small group of Poles armed with tommy guns and grenades and the much larger formations of the SS and police broke out at the wall. The outcome was not difficult to predict: several German police were killed and the wall was damaged, but two soldiers of the Polish underground movement died during the fighting, four were badly wounded, and the remainder had to retreat. Thus the first Polish combat action at the ghetto wall was of more moral than military significance. For obvious reasons, at the time I did not know the names of the soldiers of the Home Army who lost their lives in the fighting. I later found out that one of them was an eighteen-year-old student, Jozef Wilk; the other, not much older, was Eugeniusz Morawski.[11] During the following days there were more armed demonstrations of solidarity in the ghetto. A group of the communist youth shot the German crew of a heavy machine gun, and some socialist groups and a combat group of the Home Army attacked German sentries in the vicinity of the ghetto several times and assaulted the motorized units resupplying them. These attempts were paid for with additional heavy sacrifices in human life and injury.[12]

The armed resistance of the ghetto created a great deal of commotion in Warsaw. Masses of people gathered at the walls, especially in Bonifraterska Street, from where one could see the white and red flag raised beside the Jewish white and blue flag high up on one of the houses on Muranowski Square where a Jewish unit was fighting. A special assault detachment attacked the Jewish position in this section on orders of Stroop, and after a bitter fight on 20 April, it tore down the Jewish and Polish flags. "The Jewish and Polish flags were raised on a cement house as a summons to fight us," Stroop wrote in a report to General Krüger. "But both flags were captured by a special combat unit on the second day. SS-Lieutenant Dehmke died in action during the fighting with these bandits."

In the radiogram we were given to send to Dr. Ignacy Schwarzbart and Szmul Zygielbojm in London on the second day of the fighting, its authors, Feiner and Berman, stated: "Great agitation throughout the city. The population of Warsaw is following the battle with admiration and with obvious sympathy for the fighting ghetto." And the radiogram transmitted on 28 April 1943 reported:

The attitude of the defenders is creating admiration among the population of the country and humiliation and anger among the Germans. . . . Immediate successful help is now exclusively in the power of the Allies. In the name of the millions of Jews who have already been killed, in the name of those who are now being exiled and massacred, in the name of the heroic combatants, and of all of us condemned to die, we call on the whole civilized world: the mighty blow of the Allies against the bloodthirsty enemy should be dealt now in the only understandable language of revenge, and not at some time in the misty future.

Unfortunately these appeals and several others with a similar content were in vain. After a while we received a radio message from Tel Aviv addressed to the Jewish National Committee in Warsaw that had been sent by the Committee for Saving the Jews in Occupied Europe. From the Jewish Office we passed this message on to Adolf Berman. Its content was significant: "Throughout the war we have been searching for ways to establish contact with you and to give you support. Unfortunately, we are encountering unsurpassable indifference and resistance on the part of those in whose hands the possibility of saving you rests." The author of the radio message was the champion of Jewish rights and former member of the Polish parliament, Jitzchak Grünbaum. As the chairman of the committee mentioned above he vainly petitioned the representatives of the governments of the anti-Hitler coalition to take countermeasures against the German Reich and to save the surviving Polish Jews.

During the fighting in the ghetto we saw Berman and Feiner, various members of the Council for Aid to Jews, and the women who maintained contact daily and sometimes several times a day. United by a common and deeply felt sorrow, every piece of bad news from the other side of the wall touched us profoundly. Discussions of various unrealistic possibilities to save the combatants filled us with new illusions. The conditions under which we ourselves lived precluded any possibility of aid — to help was not in our power. Accordingly, we thought our most important task was to transmit news to the West regularly to keep it informed about the events in Warsaw. In addition, we attempted systematically to influence Christian Polish public opinion to win over as many people as possible who might assume the great risk of offering help and shelter to refugees. We tried to exert influence through personal contacts as well as through the underground press. We stressed the important historical and moral meaning of the ghetto uprising: this was, after all, the first rebellion of a city in the history of the European resistance movement, the first mutinous battle in the center of a major city where there was a contingent of several tens of thousands of German troops. And finally, this uprising was also a turning point in the history of the Jewish people under the occupation, a phenomenon that even surpassed the goals and expectations of the organizers and leaders of the fight themselves. I can still clearly remember the impression that Anielewicz's letter made on us. It was written on 23 April 1943, the fifth day of the fighting in the ghetto, and was addressed to his representative and friend Jitzchak Cukierman, then in the "Aryan" sector. Berman translated the letter into Polish for us:

What we are experiencing surpasses our most daring hopes. The Germans fled from the ghetto twice. . . . The most important thing is this: the dream of my life has been fulfilled — I am experiencing Jewish self-defense in the Warsaw ghetto in all its pride and glory![13]

The underground newspapers somberly directed the attention of the Christian Polish population to the heroism of the fighting Jews and appealed for its support. On 5 May 1943, while the fighting in Warsaw was still going on, the then prime minister of the Polish government in exile, General Sikorski, gave a speech on London radio and emphasized:

We are witnesses to the greatest crime in human history. We know that you are giving all the help you can to the tortured Jews. For that, my countrymen, I thank you in my own name

and in that of the government of Poland. I ask you to continue
to grant them any conceivable help and at the same time to
put a stop to this inhuman cruelty.

We printed the text of this message and disseminated
it in a flyer; in addition, we published a second flyer in
the name of the Council for Aid to Jews which combined
the words of Prime Minister Sikorski and those of an
appeal by the secret representative of the government in
the homeland concerning aid to those slated for execution. The latter had already been published at the
beginning of May 1943.

In the meantime the Germans were setting fire to one
house after another, overrunning the fortified bunkers,
killing thousands of people on the spot, and transporting
the prisoners they took to the extermination camps. During the day black clouds of smoke hung over the city,
and during the night the light of the fires illuminated the
Warsaw sky. It was like the siege of September 1939.
The initial exhilaration of the population gave way to
depression and a feeling of hopelessness.

The last report from the command of the Jewish Combat Organization (of 26 April 1943) reached us shortly
after the Easter holidays; in it Anielewicz remarks,
among other things, on the following: "Our last days
are near, but as long as we still have weapons in our
hands we will fight and offer resistance." And in fact
they did resist to the very end: until 8 May 1943, the
twentieth day of the fighting, when the Germans discovered the main bunker of the Jewish Combat
Organization.

The staff of the Jewish Combat Organization refused
to surrender to the enemy alive. Mordechai Anielewicz
and his closest associates took their own lives in the
bunker at 18 Mila Street on 8 May 1943, surrounded
by SS troops. Ten participants in the fighting in the

ghetto managed to escape with the help of Christian Poles to the "Aryan" sector through underground tunnels. Among the people rescued in this manner were the following members of the staff of the Jewish Combat Organization: Heinz Berliński, Marek Edelman, Michał Rojzenfeld, and Cywia Lubetkin. Some of this group took up arms against the Germans yet again during the general Warsaw uprising in August and September of 1944.

On 13 May 1943, Szmul Zygielbojm, an official of the "Bund" and a former Warsaw city councilman, took his own life in London. His tragic action was a protest against the silence and inaction of the world in the face of the Nazi atrocities in Poland. By that time the hopeless battle in the Warsaw ghetto had already come to an end.

On 16 May 1943 General Jürgen Stroop sent the following telegram to General Krüger in Kraków:

The former Jewish section of Warsaw no longer exists. The large-scale operation was completed with the demolition of the Warsaw synagogue at 8.15 P.M. . . . The total number of identified and exterminated Jews is 56,065.

Stroop's report on the annihilation of the Jewish quarter in Warsaw, written for the commander of the SS and the police in the *General Gouvernement* as well as for Heinrich Himmler, refers several times to the armed cooperation between Polish Christians and Jews who were fighting in the ghetto as well as to attacks on Nazi positions outside of the ghetto by "Polish bandits." In the daily reports on the fighting in the ghetto he also notes the arrest and immediate execution of Christian Poles who had been cooperating with the Jews.

After the fighting had come to an end, the Germans began the systematic destruction of the former Jewish quarter, which encompassed about forty hectares, turning it into a heap of rubble. The demolition operation was carried out with the forced labor of Hungarian, Slovak, Greek, and Polish Jewish prisoners who had been ordered there from Auschwitz and who were housed in a small camp in the depopulated area of the ghetto.

The final destruction of the ghetto was accompanied by a simultaneous intensification of the terror against the Polish intelligentsia in Warsaw and other cities within the so-called *General Gouvernement*. After the demolition of the ghetto, about 700 people (20 percent of them women) from well-known and highly respected families were incarcerated in the Gestapo prison. About fourteen days later they were executed, in the depopulated section of the ghetto, without any proof of guilt or legal proceedings. Since May of 1943 this area had become an execution ground for Christian Poles arrested by the Gestapo as well as for the Jews the Nazis tracked down in the "Aryan" sector. It was one of the repeated attempts during the years of occupation in Poland to intimidate the population and to cripple its will to resist.

These terrorist measures actually had the opposite effect of what was intended. Following the example of Warsaw, the Jewish youth of Lvov and Czestochowa started to resist the Germans in June; Bedzin followed on 3 August. On 16 September a sizable Jewish revolt took place in Białystok that was put down by the Nazis with artillery and aircraft. The unfortunate surviving inmates of the camps in Treblinka and Sobibor also decided to take action: there were armed revolts in these two death camps on 2 August and 14 October 1943. In the meantime not a week went by in Warsaw without a new attempt by the Christian Polish underground organization on the life of an official of the German police, the Gestapo, the Nazi administration, or a traitor from its own ranks. German arsenals in the city were burned, and bombs exploded in various German institutions.

Under the conditions of life during the last two years of the occupation, the most important problem for the groups concerned with aiding those Jews in hiding was to afford their charges as much protection as possible in order to increase their chances of survival. This was a task that grew increasingly more difficult from month to month. It became harder and harder to reach the ghettos and camps that still existed to supply them with money, food, and medicine.

In a report of 15 November 1943 by the Jewish National Committee to Dr. Ignacy Schwarzbart in London, Adolf Berman, Jitzchak Cukierman, and D. Kaftor wrote: "We organized our defense as well as the aid program under the indescribable conditions of a double conspiracy and amid the ragings of German terror that were also directed at the Christian Poles, while the blood of masses of executed Polish hostages was flowing in the streets every day." Those of us who were allied with the Polish independence movement, who had personal contacts with people in the Jewish underground movement and with numerous refugees from the ghettos who were seeking help, knew better than perhaps anyone else that the greatest danger to the Jews in hiding as well as to the Christian Poles who frequently offered only occasional help was that posed by criminal elements cooperating with the German police. I refer specifically to professional confidence men, informers, and blackmailers who were won over with promises of material advantages by the occupying administration. I frequently discussed this painful problem with people who, like me, were affected by it personally during the occupation. I also thought about it often after the war and researched cases of blackmail and denunciation of Jewish victims, using numerous statements by witnesses and surviving documents. I also thought about how to combat this type of crime. And it is my deepest conviction that, even though there were not as many informers as is generally assumed, they caused a disproportional amount of damage in relation to their numbers because of their mobility and their criminal initiative as well as because of their efficient organization within a kind of network.

Thanks to an especially fortunate coincidence and the courage of people unknown to me, I myself managed to avoid being denounced to the Warsaw Gestapo during the summer of 1944. A postal employee, whom I have not met to this very day, accepted and opened a letter in a post office in Warsaw that was addressed to the Gestapo. In it, the addressee accused me of participating in the assistance program for the Jews and gave my first and last name as well as my address. Based on the address in the denunciation, the letter was forwarded to me in my home. I naturally changed my apartment immediately to forestall any additional efforts by the anonymous informer and reported the matter to my superiors in the Home Army.

Perhaps the informer would have been found out in time, but the rebellion in Warsaw began a few days later, on 1 August 1944, making any action in the matter impossible.

The blackmailers, called *szmalcownik*, played just as infamous a role as the informers. They extorted money and valuables by threatening to denounce their victims to the German police. The Jews thus driven from their hiding places were frequently left destitute. They were obliged immediately to change their place of residence and the papers they had been using. I was frequently faced with the necessity of providing prompt assistance to people who had become victims of blackmailers.

To put an end to this criminal activity and to warn all who were tempted to commit the sin of Cain against their fellow Jewish citizens, either through thoughtlessness or the influence of corrupting individuals, the underground Leadership of the Civil Resistance, which enjoyed great authority in occupied Poland, published a declaration in March of 1943, the time of the most intense Nazi terror against the Jews and of the final liquidation of many ghettos:

Even though it is itself a victim of the shocking terror, the Christian Polish population views the slaughter of the remaining Jewish inhabitants of Poland by the Germans with horror and the deepest compassion. It has protested against this crime, and its protest has been heard throughout the free world. The Christian Polish population has helped the Jews who fled from the ghettos or managed to escape from the camps to such an extent that the occupying forces published a proclamation which threatened every Christian Pole who helped a Jew in hiding with death. Unfortunately, a few infamous, unscrupulous people with roots in the criminal world have surfaced who have discovered a malicious source of income by blackmailing not only the Jews, but their Christian Polish compatriots who have hidden them as well.

The Leadership of the Civil Combat Organization will record all of these extortions and prosecute them now to the full extent of the law within the given conditions, and will do so under all circumstances in the future.

— The Leadership of the Civil Combat Organization

This declaration, which was in complete agreement with the demands of the Council for Aid to Jews, was published in the widely circulated underground press of the Home Army, in the official publication of the government, and in the various democratic underground journals. Soon after its publication the head of the Civil Combat Organization, the lawyer Stefan Korbonski, during the course of a conference of the regional leaders of the entire country, recommended strict punishment of the informers and extortionists threatening the Jews and the Christian Poles helping them.[14]

On 30 April 1943, at a time when the fighting in the Warsaw ghetto was still going on, the presiding delegate of the Polish government published a long statement that concluded as follows:

The political leadership of the country has already expressed its deeply felt abhorrence of the German crimes against the Jews and emphatically repeats its condemnation of these horrendous deeds. The Christian Polish community is right to demonstrate compassion for the hunted and persecuted Jews and to help them. It should continue to offer this help.

In addition, we published leaflets addressed to the Polish people in May, August, and September of 1943, in the name of the Council for Aid to Jews. These were signed "The Polish Independence Organizations." They made special reference to the moral value of "actions and heroic deeds intended to save human beings from the beast Hitler." These leaflets were placed in the entrances of large apartment buildings, mailed out, and posted on walls. Referring to the prosecution of Nazi criminals and to cases of collaboration with the Germans several weeks later in a common declaration of 5 July 1943, the leading civilian and military institutions of the Polish underground noted categorically that "all cases of extortion and the enticing of money under the pretext of freeing prisoners or interned Poles as well as the extortion of money from Jews living in hiding are subject to criminal prosecution by special courts."

The Jewish office of the delegation of the Polish government received the first reports of blackmail soon thereafter. We passed these on to the intelligence units that specifically, one could say professionally, dealt with

BEKANNTMACHUNG

Betr.: Todesstrafe für Unterstützung von Juden, die die jüdischen Wohnbezirke unbefugt verlassen haben.

In der letzten Zeit haben sich zahlreiche Juden aus den ihnen zugewiesenen jüdischen Wohnbezirken unbefugt entfernt. Sie halten sich z. Zt. noch im Distrikt Warschau auf.

Ich weise darauf hin, dass durch die Dritte Verordnung des Generalgouverneurs über Aufenthaltsbeschränkung im Generalgouvernement vom 15.10.1941 (VBl. GG. S. 595) nicht nur die Juden, die in dieser Weise unbefugt den ihnen zugewiesenen Wohnbezirk verlassen haben, mit dem Tode bestraft werden, sondern dass die gleiche Strafe jeden trifft, der solchen Juden wissentlich Unterschlupf gewährt. Dazu gehört nicht nur die Gewährung von Nachtlager und Verpflegung, sondern auch jede anderweitige Unterstützung, z. B. durch Mitnahme in Fahrzeugen aller Art, durch Ankauf jüdischer Sachwerte usw.

Ich richte hiermit an die Bevölkerung des Distrikts Warschau die Aufforderung, jeden Juden, der sich unbefugt ausserhalb eines jüdischen Wohnbezirks aufhält, sofort dem nächsten Polizeirevier oder Gendarmerieposten zu melden.

Wer einem Juden Unterstützung hat zuteil werden lassen oder z. Zt. noch zuteil werden lässt, hiervon aber bis zum 9.9.42 18 Uhr, der nächsten polizeilichen Dienststelle Mitteilung macht, wird STRAFRECHTLICH NICHT VERFOLGT WERDEN.

In der gleichen Weise wird gegen denjenigen von einer Strafverfolgung Abstand genommen, der die von einem Juden erworbenen Sachwerte bis zum 9.9.42, 18 Uhr, in Warschau, Niskastr. 20, abliefert oder bei dem nächsten Polizeirevier bzw. Gendarmerieposten Meldung erstattet.

Warschau, den 5. September 1942.

Der SS- und Polizeiführer im Distrikt Warschau.

8. Anyone who offered aid to Jews faced the death penalty. (See pages 37–38 for a complete translation of the document.)

REPUBLIC OF POLAND

Ministry of Foreign Affairs

THE MASS EXTERMINATION
of JEWS in
GERMAN OCCUPIED POLAND

NOTE
**addressed to the Governments of the
United Nations on December 10th, 1942,
and other documents**

*Published on behalf of the Polish
Ministry of Foreign Affairs by*

HUTCHINSON & CO. (Publishers) LTD.
LONDON : NEW YORK : MELBOURNE
Price: Threepence Net.

9. The Polish government in exile in London attempted to galvanize the conscience of the world and to goad the countries represented in the United Nations into action with a report to that body entitled *The Mass Extermination of Jews in German Occupied Poland* and through other diplomatic actions. Pictured is the front cover of this document from early in 1943.

10. The artillery of the German *Wehrmacht* bombarding the Warsaw ghetto (April 1943).

11. The "large-scale operation" involved in suppressing the Warsaw ghetto uprising was led by SS-*Brigadeführer* and head of the police Jürgen Stroop, shown third from the left.

12. People on fire jump out of windows: a photograph from the Stroop Report.

13. People dragged from cellars awaiting the decision of their captors: a photograph from the Stroop Report.

14. Captured women of the Jewish Combat Organization: a photograph from the Stroop Report.

15. From the last days of the Warsaw ghetto uprising. The captured civilians, including women and children, were shot or taken to concentration camps.

16. Civilians are taken to their deaths through the burning streets of the Warsaw ghetto. A photograph from the last days of the uprising.

17. "The large-scale operation was completed . . . with the demolition of the Warsaw synagogue at 8:15 P.M."—from the Stroop Report.

18. "For . . . sheltering Jews . . . the following . . . were sentenced to death"—a notice of 17 December 1943. (See page 111 for a partial translation of the document.)

19. The tree planted on behalf of the underground Council for Aid to Jews (1942–44), which went under the code name *Zegota*, on the Mount of Remembrance in Jerusalem.

20. A memorial tablet with inscriptions in Hebrew and French is attached to the tree. Among the names it lists is that of the author of this book.

these matters. After a short time the first death sentences were being passed on German and Polish informants and officials of the security police who had specialized in denouncing or blackmailing hidden Jews. It must be noted that tracking down the guilty was by no means easy. From my own experience I know that the information obtained from people who had themselves been victims of blackmail (and as a consequence of robbery) was generally not sufficient to find an extortionist in a city of millions. Naturally, it could hardly be expected that the frightened victims would know the name and address of their tormentors. Thus we had to use a different method. We obtained our information directly from Christian Poles who worked for the security police with the knowledge of and under orders from the underground organizations. In this way we managed to unmask several dozen confidence men whose cases were turned over to the special court.

The sentences passed on traitors by the special courts were carried out by young, self-sacrificing men acting for the underground Polish government at great personal risk. In order to prepare for the assassination of a police functionary or informer it was frequently necessary to wait about for hours in the streets or in entrance ways guarded by the Germans to observe the person in question and to get close to him at the appropriate moment. In spite of careful planning in assassinations of this kind, incidents similar to the one that took place during the execution of the sentence on Willy Leitgeber, a member of the Gestapo who was known for his brutality toward Jews and Christian Poles, sometimes occurred. The assassination was set for an afternoon in June of 1944 amid the heavy traffic of central Warsaw. As expected, Leitgeber appeared at a certain location; contrary to expectations, however, he was not alone, but in the company of seven other Nazi officials. A general shoot-out

ensued, during which Leitgeber as well as some of the other Gestapo men were killed. I can remember the well-known execution of a confidence man, a Pole named Tadeusz Karcz, who had specialized in denouncing and blackmailing Jews, in a busy cafe on Nowy-Swiat Street, one of the main streets of Warsaw. The member of the Home Army who was to execute Karcz in November of 1943 shot him at a table in the cafe in a room in which several German officers were also present. Two companions of the executioner kept the officers in check with their tommy guns. We suffered no losses, and a few days later the underground press published a short report on the execution of a death sentence for "delivering Polish citizens of Jewish nationality into the hands of the Germans." This was sufficient explanation of the mysterious shots in the cafe that the whole city was talking about.

Generally, those who carried out death sentences had to bring all of the documents and papers they found on the condemned person to their superiors. During the fall of 1943 I came into the possession of a notebook that had been found on Borys Pilnik, who had been executed in a holiday resort near Warsaw in the summer of 1943. Pilnik was the leader of a whole group of blackmailers who hunted down Jews living in the "Aryan" sector, including people who were married to non-Jews. They would then force these unfortunate people to pay for their silence. This criminal's notebook was a veritable record of his heinous deeds. In it he had carefully noted the names, and in some cases the addresses, of the people who had been blackmailed so far, and he had pedantically entered records of the amounts of extorted money. In addition, it contained names and addresses of people who were potential victims for blackmail or denunciation, some of which were followed by a question mark. For example, it read: "The daughter of the Rabbi?" followed by the address, or, "Mixed marriage? —needs

to be investigated," or the initials and address of an unknown person with the addition: "Valuables." When we were able to find the victims, we informed them immediately and told them that their tormentor was no longer alive. For a while they would be safe. We also warned the other people that the names they lived under in the "Aryan" sector had become known to an extortionist and that they thus might be known to other members of the group. At the time we made several copies of the contents of the notebook in the Jewish office of the government delegation. These copies survived the later destruction of Warsaw. (I later saw one in the archives of Yad Vashem in Jerusalem in 1963.)

The struggle against the blackmailers was exceedingly difficult. It was nevertheless carried out systematically as far as possible by the Polish underground organizations during 1943 and 1944. If, however — as events would show in several cases — the memory of the wrongs and the personal tragedies suffered as a consequence of denunciation was stronger and more lasting in those who were rescued than the memory of the incomparibly more numerous cases of proffered assistance, this has to be regarded as a characteristic, but also understandable, trait of human nature. In general, tragic and negative experiences leave a deeper and more lasting impression on the human psyche than do good and positive ones.

Aside from the German police and the informers and extortionists, who were recruited from the dregs of the Christian Polish and Ukrainian populations, it was the Jewish confidence men who represented the greatest threat to Jews living in hiding. Seduced by false hopes and promises, they frequently helped the Germans to track down fellow Jews who were in hiding in the "Aryan" sector. The Jewish underground organizations had already declared a relentless war on these traitors when the ghetto still existed and killed them without mercy. But there were more complicated forms of cooperation with the occupying forces that were not always dictated by evil intent, but were rather the result of a harmful confusion. The infamous case of the "legal emigration" of Jews from Poland with South American passports in 1943 is an example of this. The matter caused us much concern and finally had a tragic outcome. Several South American republics, especially Paraguay, offered citizenship to a number of Jews who had by that time been murdered in the ghettos. To summarize the subsequent events I will quote the original text from the "Report of the Central Committee of the 'Bund' " of 15 November 1943. This was signed "Berezowski" (the cover name of Leon Feiner) and passed through my hands before being sent on to the representative of the "Bund" in London, Dr. Emanuel Scherer:

A large number of the letters that were sent to the consulates of Paraguay and Switzerland for Jews who had by then been murdered in the German-controlled ghettos in Poland . . . became an object of barter in the hands of despicable Jewish confidence men in the employ of the Gestapo. People were occasionally enticed to pay enormous sums for them. In certain uneducable Jewish circles these letters came to be regarded as a ticket to freedom and safety, as a letter of safe conduct. . . . Helpless in the face of extermination, a psychosis spread among the desperate Jews that was consciously encouraged by the Gestapo's Jewish confidence men. . . . It did not take very long for this new and tragic illusion to be shattered. At the time that the third group was to leave for that longed-for paradise — the foreigners' camp near Hannover — more than three hundred Jews were arrested and shot. . . .

As chance would have it, I was able to observe directly the lamentable end of these attempts at emigration using papers from neutral countries. Dozens of Jewish families who had thus far avoided discovery went to two collection points in Warsaw that had been established in hotels requisitioned in 1943 by the German police for this specific purpose. The Jewish families were treated decently in the hotels, which strengthened their false assumption that the Germans would be true to their word. I was watching one of the hotels around noon on 13 July 1943 when several large German trucks drove up. About three hundred Jewish men, women, and children were loaded into the trucks with their personal belongings in front of the building. This was actually done in a friendly manner. I could hardly suppress my astonishment at the sight of Germans helping women and the elderly into the trucks — after all, this took place after the horrors of the extermination of the ghettos. The gruesome comedy was played out to its end. After a quarter of an hour it was clear that the loaded trucks were driving in the direction of the Gestapo prison on Dzielna Street. The next day I contacted one of the prison guards, a Polish woman and co-conspirator in the underground, who gave me the comforting news that the majority of the people brought from the hotel had been placed in normal prison cells with the explanation that their papers were faulty. On the following day, the same guard informed me that about three hundred people in possession of foreign passports had been executed in the ruins of the ghetto. I made an initial oral and then written report of this tragic news, corroborating our worst fears, to Leon Feiner and Adolf Berman, the Jewish representatives in the underground organizations of Warsaw. This report is among the few archival documents that have survived relating to the cooperation between the Polish Christian and Jewish underground movements in Warsaw during the occupation. At present it is located in the municipal archives in Warsaw.

Along with the constant, one is tempted to say routine, activities of material and moral support for the Jews living in hiding and the transmission abroad of information and reports of the events in occupied Poland, we thought it necessary to influence the Christian Polish population in various ways by making them aware of the details of the Jewish tragedy. We also wanted to create circumstances that were as advantageous as possible for the programs executed by the Council for Aid to Jews, by the Jewish Office of the Government Delegacy, by the Jewish Office of the military organizations, and by the other centers of the Polish underground movement. This undertaking, which had as its goal to inform, persuade, and educate the public, was by no means limited to the publication of leaflets calling for the support of Jews. It was also carried out through the underground press and, above all, through special publications released jointly by Polish Christians and Jews in the form of pamphlets dedicated to topical events. It would be wrong not to mention these important journalistic activities here, but I will limit myself to a few examples. In May 1943, when the fighting in the ghetto was coming to an end, a Polish Girl Scout of my acquaintance, Maria Kann, who was then beginning her career as a writer, approached me and asked me to help her obtain documents she needed for work on a publication about the events in the ghetto which she intended as an "Appeal to the Conscience of the World." I gave her copies of the bulletins and radio messages of the Jewish organizations that had been sent abroad, as well as of reports on the activities of the Jewish Combat Organization that had mainly been supplied to the Jewish office of the Government Delegacy by Adolf Berman. Based on these and other materials, the author wrote a relatively long pamphlet entitled "Before the Eyes of the World." It was printed in secret in Warsaw during the summer of 1943. During the fall of 1943 I was already involved in distributing the pamphlet, of which 2,100 copies had been printed. "Before the Eyes of the World" is not only deeply disturbing because of the events it describes, but above all because of the deeply human comments that point out the incredible moral danger to humanity represented by its indifference to the extermination of a whole people.

"A people was murdered before the eyes of the world, before our eyes, before the eyes of our youth," Maria Kann wrote.

We watched inactively. In spite of all our indignation we grew accustomed to the idea that killing is permissible, that you can build crematories for living human beings. The idea that there are different kinds of people takes seed in the minds of children. 'Master,' 'servants,' and finally 'dogs' that you can kill without punishment. This is the horrendous legacy left by the bloodthirsty Führer. . . . Sometime the world will cease to be a slaughterhouse. Order and peace will return. And many years later a child will ask: Did they kill a human being or a Jew, Mother?

At the beginning of 1944 two additional underground publications with similar messages appeared in Warsaw. One of the two dealt with the shocking experiences of Jankiel Wiernik, a Jew who had fled from Treblinka. He wrote it after his successful escape from that death camp and it was published by the Coordination Committee of the Jewish underground organizations (the Zionist organizations and the "Bund") then active in Poland. I participated in the distribution of the pamphlet, published under the title "One Year in Treblinka," and arranged for it to be given to a courier of the underground movement who was departing for London. The second publication was an anthology of poems entitled *From the Abyss*, which contained poems by eleven Polish Christian and Jewish writers. Along with works by Mieczysław Jastrun and Czesław Miłosz, it contained poems by less well known authors such as Michał Borwicz and Tadeusz Sarnecki, who expressed thoughts similar to those of their more famous contemporaries. Sarnecki also wrote the poetic dedication of this anthology. Its opening words clearly delineated its intent: "I dedicate this flaming hymn to those who had courage: to the Jews of Warsaw fighting against the superior strength of the enemy."

All of the poems were dedicated to the tragedy of the extermination of the Polish Jews. We succeeded in smuggling the anthology out of the country; it was published in the United States while the war was still going on and soon thereafter in Palestine, where it was translated into Hebrew. The impression that the words of these poets of a dying people made in the free world in 1944, as well as the extent to which they were in accord with other Polish poets, are reflected in the following passage, published in the United States, by the Polish author Jozef Witlin:

The hand shakes, the mouth goes dry, the breath falters — when we read these poems. Shame burns the eyes as they glide along the black mournful lines of these pages, beautiful even though filled with bitterness. The eyes are ashamed to be reading these sung relics of destruction and heroism, ashamed that they can read and not go blind. The words from which this poetry blossoms are the same Polish words that human beings use to communicate with the living. And still we believe that this is the language of people whom God has already consoled.

I and the other members of the Council for Aid to Jews distributed this book of poems for several months.

Through what I observed, I can attest that it made a great contribution to awakening the conscience of and imparting a deeper understanding of the tragedy of the Jewish people in young intellectuals and students.

I would like to conclude these memories of the years of horror, which must naturally be limited in scope, with the following experience. Among the most valuable experiences of my life in the years after the war was the moment when, in October of 1963, following the lighting of the eternal fire in the crypt on the Mount of Remembrance (Har Hazikaron) in Jerusalem (by Yad Vashem)[15] beside the symbolic grave in which the ashes of the Jewish victims of the Nazi concentration camps are enshrined, I heard the affirmation, spoken in Hebrew and then repeated in Polish, that concludes with the following words:

> We remember the heroic deeds of the fighters of the ghetto, the underground fighters, the partisans, and the soldiers who heeded the rallying cry to do battle against the far superior forces of the enemy to salvage the honor of their people. We remember those who defended their humanity with honor and steadfastness; those who gave aid to the Jews in the name of the most holy human ideals and at the risk of their own lives.

At the time I thought of all my friends and colleagues, Polish Jews and Christians, with whom I had the honor to work for a cause that not only involved the duty of saving human lives, but also the opportunity to save our own human dignity.

Today, the awareness that uncountable numbers of human beings were the victims of a planned campaign of racial hatred stands as a testament to the suffering and martyrdom, to the tears and the blood of the victims of the Warsaw ghetto and of the death camps. The meaning of the existence of the great human family can in

the long run only be preserved by attempting to overcome everything that separates us — through an active
defense of the inalienable right of every human being to
a life free from fear, and through the public recollection
of what bound and binds us together.

Epilogue: Forty Years Later

DURING THE FORTY YEARS that have gone by since the end of the war, I have retained a vivid memory of all of the events I witnessed, and my thoughts often return to the people on both sides of the ghetto wall with whom I was so intimately connected during that tragic period. As far as possible, I have kept in touch with the Jews and Christian Poles whose lives were as decisively changed by the events of that time as mine was. As a publisher, author, historian, and teacher at a university, my work has repeatedly revolved around questions of the fate and the experience of people during the Second World War. I have lectured about the war in Poland, as well as in Israel, England, America, and Germany. The fact that I was a conscious witness to the events has frequently aroused great interest in my audiences, and I have been inundated with questions that spring from a desire to understand matters that all too frequently do not lend themselves to rational explanation. One is left with a vague, completely inadequate attempt to imagine these human fates.

After this book was published on the fortieth anniversary of the heroic and tragic Warsaw ghetto uprising, readers of the mid and younger generations frequently asked me about the lives of the people who were mentioned only in passing in the book. It is not easy to satisfy this interest, for nearly every one of the Polish Jews and

Christians I met during the war could be the hero of his or her own story. And many of the real experiences in occupied Poland — whether in Warsaw or Kraków, in the ghetto or beyond its walls, in the Christian or the Jewish resistance, in the prisons or the camps — could be the basis for a screenplay or for extensive literary research. And the majority of these events could certainly be the starting point for ethical, psychological, or historical-philosophical reflections and meditations, and above all for the exploration of the philosophical question, What is humanity and what can it be?

But I will limit myself to a few short notes on the fate of the most important people mentioned in this book.

Only a few of the people who participated in and organized the Jewish resistance in Poland lived to see the end of the war. Jozef Kapłan was arrested by the Gestapo in 1942 and paid for his fight for freedom and dignity with his life. Mordechai Tenenbaum died in 1943. Szmul Breslaw did survive the Warsaw ghetto uprising in 1943, but was killed a year later when he took part in the great Warsaw uprising that began in August of 1944 and was intended to free the capital of Poland.

Of the members of the first staff of the Zionist-socialist combat organization that was founded in the Warsaw ghetto in July of 1942, Jitzchak Cukierman and his wife Cywia Lubetkin survived those days of horror. They both left Poland soon after the war was over and emigrated to Israel, where they became well known and well respected. For thirty years they lived in the kibbutz of Lohamei Haghettaot ("Heros of the Warsaw Ghetto") in Galilee in the vicinity of Naharia and Akko. I visited them there while I was staying in Israel in 1963. They had been energetic supporters of a research center with an accompanying museum and archive that was built in their kibbutz. The center is mainly dedicated to the history of the Warsaw ghetto and the Jewish resistance in Poland during the Second World War, and is named after Jitzchak Kacenelson, a Warsaw Jew, educator, and poet, who was murdered in a Nazi concentration camp. Kacenelson's main contribution to the literary history of the time is his horrifying poem "Song of the Murdered Jewish People." Cywia Lubetkin died on 13 July 1978; Jitzchak Cukierman on 17 June 1981.

Arie Wilner (code name "Jurek"), who appears frequently in my book, took his own life on 8 May 1943 together with Mordechai Anielewicz to avoid surrendering to his enemies. He was in a hopeless situation, surrounded by the SS in the bunker in the Warsaw ghetto together with several fellow combatants. His father and his sister Gusta Wilner, who had also been active in the resistance, survived the war and later lived in Tel Aviv.

Marek Edelman, who as the delegate of the "Bund" was on the staff of the Jewish Combat Organization, as well as a representative of Anielewicz and an organizer and leader of the fighting in the Warsaw ghetto in April and May of 1943, completed his medical studies in Poland after the war. Today he is a highly respected heart specialist in Łódź. He is one of the best-known people in Poland and is held in high esteem for his exemplary conduct as a physician and especially for his human qualities — his generosity, his straightforwardness, and his remarkable civil courage. He was very active in the Solidarity movement in 1980–81. Since the death of Jitzchak Cukierman, Marek Edelman is the sole surviving leader of the Jewish resistance in Poland during World War II. The lawyer Leon Feiner (born in 1888), vice-president of the secret Council for Aid to Jews, died of cancer on 22 February 1945. He did not see the end of the war, but he did die as a free man since the Germans were already on the retreat and had vacated parts of Poland.

After the war the psychologist Doctor Adolf Berman (born in 1906) and his wife Barbara at first lived in Warsaw, where Berman was the chairman of the Jewish Central Committee in Poland. A few years later they emigrated to Israel. There Berman became a representative of the leftist-socialist Mapam Party in the Knesset. Later he joined the Communist Party of Israel. In spite of differences in political opinions he was respected in Israel and in Jewish circles throughout the world for his actions during the war. His wife Barbara died in 1953. Berman himself died in Tel Aviv twenty-five years later, on 3 March 1978. He showed warm friendship toward anyone who had experienced the fateful years of the war with him. In 1963 in Tel Aviv he gave me the manuscript of a report. It was intended for publication in one of my books and opened with the following words: "The time for the Great Golden Book of the Christian Poles who reached out a helping hand to the Jews and saved them from death during the terrible 'period of contempt' will come. They became an elevating symbol of humanity and solidarity to the Jewish underground movement."

At this point I should perhaps mention that the two prominent professors from the University of Warsaw, Stanisław Ossowski and Maria Ossowska, who arranged for me to meet with Berman in the fall of 1942, also survived the war. Stanisław Ossowski died in November 1963; Maria Ossowska in August 1974 in Warsaw.

Most of the important, respected, and active organizers of the Council for Aid to Jews of Poland are no longer with us. However, the lawyer Stanisław Dobrowolski, a socialist and former chairman of the Council for Aid to Jews in Kraków, and Irena Sendlerowa, a retired teacher who distinguished herself through her aid to Jewish children, still live in Warsaw. The journalist

Miriam Peleg, who as Maria Hochberg-Marianska was
very active in the Christian Polish and Jewish resistance
in Kraków, lives in Tel Aviv. And finally, the author of
these words, whose permanent residence is in Warsaw
and who is temporarily in West Germany, is also still
alive. But the two organizers of the Council for Aid to
Jews in occupied Poland, Zofia Kossak-Szatkowska
(born in 1892) and Wanda Krahelska-Filipowicz (born
in 1886), both died in 1968. The first chairman of the
Council, the socialist Julian Grobelny (born in 1893),
died of tuberculosis in December 1944. The vice-chair-
man of the Council, Tadeusz Rek (born in 1906), died
in Warsaw on 11 November 1968, the Council's treasurer Fredynand Marek-Arczynski (born in 1900) on 16
February 1979, and the head of the office and of the
secretaries' pool, Zofia Rudnicka (Lusia Hausman), on
7 February 1981.

The founder and president of the Council in Lvov,
Wladysława Chomsowa, the widow of a major, spent
the first years after the war in London as a political
emigré, then, at the urging of her friends, she relocated
to Israel. She died in Haifa in 1966 and was buried there.

The numbers of intellectuals who played such an important role in collecting and processing information on
the Jewish situation in occupied Poland and in passing
it on to the West, have also been greatly diminished.
The famous historian Stanisław Herbst, who taught at
the University of Warsaw after the war, died on 24 June
1973. Aleksander Kaminski, a scholar of the theory and
history of education and professor emeritus at the University of Łódź, died on 15 March 1978. But the most
recent to die, on 12 March 1986, was Kattowitz Henryk
Woliński, a lawyer and formerly the head of the Jewish
contingent of the Home Army. After Woliński's death
the following obituary appeared in one of Warsaw's
dailies: "On 12 March 1986 Henryk Woliński — 'Wac-

taw' — passed on. I wish to acknowledge my deepest respect for him in the name of all of the soldiers of the Jewish Combat Organization. — Marek Edelman."

Maria Kann in Warsaw, Michał Borwicz in Paris, and Czesław Miłosz in Berkeley, the recipient of the 1980 Nobel Prize for literature, are among the writers still living who described the suffering, death, and resistance of the Polish Jews during the period of the "final solution" in prose or poetry in the underground publications of the resistance movement.

The unprecedented Jewish tragedy during the years of the Second World War, the attempt utterly to annihilate the people of Abraham and Isaac, was mainly the doing of Christians. The actions of these people made a mockery of the fifth commandment and the commandment to love one's neighbor. But they were Europeans, people who were born and grew up in a part of the world where ethical values had crystallized in an environment of Christian morality and traditions. For more than forty years the crime that has been recorded in history as the "final solution to the Jewish question" has been occupying the consciences and thoughts of philosophers, psychologists, sociologists, historians, and all who possess a certain amount of moral sensitivity. The question arises again and again: How could it happen, and what does it mean both for humanity and for the individual?

When I was writing this book I felt obliged to state the truth by referring to the events I myself experienced in the city of Warsaw on the Vistula in Europe. I know that the annihilation of the Jews is the special and direct responsibility of the perpetrators of the crime. But it is also an indirect responsibility of everyone who committed the sin of inaction: of indifference, small-mindedness, and cowardice.

By now there are several thousand carob trees growing along the Avenue of the Just among the Peoples of the

World in Jerusalem. Planted in 1962, they are symbolic reminders of people of many nationalities — known as well as unknown — who followed the call of their conscience during those horrible years, who overcame their fear and helped save the lives of the condemned Jews. The medals given to those so honored have these words engraved on them: "Whoever saves a life saves the whole world." Growing beside the Dutch, Danish, and French trees are about 1,500 trees with plaques bearing Polish names. Many of the names in this book can be found there. There are also trees with the names of people from Germany and Austria.

When God threatened to destroy Sodom because of the outrages in that city, Abraham pleaded for its inhabitants. God's response was that he would spare the city for the sake of only ten just people (Gen. 18:32). I tend to think that the people who, during the Second World War, were able to combat Nazi crimes and those who, having been saved from destruction, remind us of these acts of human solidarity, made and make a contribution toward assuring that the world after Auschwitz will not be completely without hope.

W.B.

Notes

1. These were hiding places, both above and below ground, constructed by Jews living in the ghetto—ED.

2. The *General Gouvernement* was a state, which included Warsaw, created by the Germans in the center of occupied Poland. No Pole was allowed to cross the borders of the *General Gouvernement* without permission from the German authorities—ED.

3. Karnibad was arrested by the Gestapo in October 1943 and executed a few days later.

4. Piekalkiewicz, arrested by the Gestapo in February of 1943, was tortured to death during his interrogation.

5. The first of these decrees, instituted by Hans Frank, was published on 15 October 1941. The following Nazi officials affirmed the death penalty for providing aid to Jews: Ferdinand von Sammern Frankenegg, chief of the SS and police in the District of Warsaw, on 5 September 1942; Dr. Boettcher, head of the SS and police in the District of Radom, on 25 September 1942; and Friedrich Krüger, chief of the SS and police in the *General Gouvernement*. In his directive of 28 October 1942, Krüger went even farther by making the failure to inform the German police of a Jew discovered to be in hiding — in other words, refusal to cooperate with the extermination apparatus — a crime (which in practical terms meant imprisonment in a concentration camp for the offender): "Security measures will be invoked against those who are aware of the unauthorized presence of a Jew outside of a Jewish residential area and who do not report this to the police." Boettcher stated

publicly that this decree was based on the established fact that the Polish population was sheltering Jews.

6. The following were represented in the committee: the Zionist groups Po'alei Zion, Hechaluz, Hashomer Haztair, Dror, Akiba, and Gordonia.

7. This order came to light after the war and was addressed to Friedrich Krüger, commanding officer of the SS and police in the *General Gouvernement*. In it Himmler states: "An over-all plan for the destruction of the ghetto is to be prepared. What must be achieved at all costs is the complete destruction of the present living space of 500,000 *Untermenschen*, as this living space will never be fit for Germans, and that the area of the city of Warsaw, which as a source of decay and resistance is an ever-increasing menace, be diminished.

8. Klepfisz was killed on the second day of the ghetto uprising during heavy fighting with a detachment of the SS and Nazi police. The high command of the Polish armed forces decorated him posthumously with its highest combat honor, the Virtuti Militari distinguished service medal.

9. This was the apartment of Bogna Domanska (niece of the great Polish writer of Jewish descent Benedikt Hertz), who was one of the most courageous and unselfish women I worked with. Domanska was the secretary of the Jewish Office and an invaluable aide in the work of the Council for Aid to Jews. She now lives in England.

10. Captain Pszenny later took part in many battles against the Germans, as well as in the Warsaw uprising. He now lives and works in Chicago. His brother, who was wounded in the fight described, lives in Warsaw.

11. The parents and sister of Jozef Wilk are still living in Poland. No member of Morawski's family survived the war. There is a portrait of the two victims in the museum of the Jewish Historical Institute in Warsaw.

12. Stroop's infamous report, published after the war, confirms these facts: there are several references to "Polish bandits" working together with the Jews, as well as to Polish combat activity at the ghetto wall, and even to the arrest and "immediate execution" of thirty-five Poles who were sup-

porting the ghetto with weapons brought in from the "Aryan" sector.

13. The Nazis regarded the situation created by the armed ghetto uprising as quite serious. On 20 April 1943 Hans Frank, head of the *General Gouvernement*, informed Hans Lammers, chief of Hitler's chancellery: "Since yesterday we have experienced a well-organized revolt in the ghetto that has required the use of heavy guns."

14. Korbonski now lives in Washington, D.C. He is one of the Poles who today bears the title "Just among the Peoples of the World."

15. "Yad Vashem," a phrase from the book of Isaiah (56:5), means "a monument and a name." Yad Vashem is one of the organizations instituted in Jerusalem by the Israeli Knesset both for the Jewish victims of Nazism in Europe and as a monument to peace. Among other things, the institute is responsible for collecting documentary material on Jews everywhere in order that their struggle and revolt against the Nazis and their collaborators will not be forgotten. The institute established the title "Just among the Peoples of the World" for those who risked their lives in order to help the Jews.

Appendix: Translation of Documents Shown in the Illustrations

[Illus. 1]

DIRECTIVE
concerning the
Identification of Jews
in the District of Warsaw

Effective 1 December 1939, I hereby order that all Jews over the age of twelve in the District of Warsaw shall wear a visible identifying badge whenever they are outside their own place of residence. This directive also applies to Jews temporarily within the District for the duration of their stay.

This directive defines as a Jew:

1. anyone who belongs, or has belonged, to the Mosaic faith;

2. anyone whose father or mother belongs, or has belonged, to the Mosaic faith.

The identifying badge must be worn in the form of an armband on the upper right arm of the clothing or overgarment, and shall consist of a blue star of David against a white background. The white background must be large enough that the points of the overlying star are at least eight centimeters apart.

The bars from which the star is constructed must be at least one centimeter wide.

Jews who fail to meet this obligation will be subject to severe punishment.

The Council of Elders will be responsible for carrying out this directive, particularly with regard to supplying the Jews with identifying badges.

Within the city of Warsaw, execution of this directive is incumbent upon the mayor, and in the surrounding area upon local officials.

Chief Officer of the District of Warsaw
Dr. Fischer
Governor

[Illus. 6]

Notice

Concerning: The death penalty for unauthorized departure from the Jewish quarter.

The recent outbreak of typhus is in many cases directly attributable to the Jews who have left their assigned district. In order to protect the population, the governor has ordered that, in the future, any Jew who leaves his or her assigned district without authorization will be sentenced to death.

The same punishment will apply to anyone who knowingly grants refuge to these Jews, or who aids them in any other way (e.g., by providing lodging, food, transportation in vehicles of any sort, etc.).

This sentence will be carried out through the Warsaw Special Court.

Appendix

I expressly draw the attention of the entire populace to this new regulation, which will be enforced with the greatest severity.

Warsaw, 10 November 1941

signed, Dr. Fischer
Governor

[Illus. 7]

The Commissar
of the Jewish Quarter
in Warsaw

Notice

For leaving the Jewish quarter of Warsaw without authorization, the following Jews . . . by judgment of the Warsaw Special Court on 12 November 1941, were sentenced to death.
The sentence was carried out on 17 November 1941.

signed, Auerswald

[Illus. 18]

Notice

For offenses committed — namely, for membership in an illegal organization, aiding criminals, sheltering Jews, possession of weapons, failure to report possession of weapons, and dissemination of handbills — the following Jews, in police court-martial and in pursuance of sections 1 and 2 of the order of 2 October 1943, were sentenced to death. . . .

Index

Index

Index

Index